CAIRO PAPERS IN SOCIAL SCIENCE

VOLUME 35   NUMBER 4

On Friendship between the No Longer and the Not Yet

An Ethnographic Account

Soha Mohsen

THE AMERICAN UNIVERSITY IN CAIRO PRESS

CAIRO   NEW YORK

Cover photo: courtesy of Tasneem Gad

This paperback edition first published in 2023 by
The American University in Cairo Press
113 Sharia Kasr el Aini, Cairo, Egypt
420 Lexington Avenue, Suite 1644, New York, NY 10170
www.aucpress.com

First published in an electronic edition in 2020

ISBN 978 1 649 03229 4

Library of Congress Cataloging-in-Publication Data applied for

1 2 3 4 5   27 26 25 24

Designed by Adam el-Sehemy

Contents

Acknowledgments

To Dr. Hanan Sabea, the mentor, the shining star, and the friend who accompanied me for two and a half years through the most exhilarating ride of my life. I remember September 2015 when it all started, her voice and her glimmering eyes, her encounters with the joys and dramas of the everyday. She taught me that it all matters. Hanan's engagement with classic and contemporary anthropologists, philosophers, and thinkers, alive or dead, near or far, taught me that a conversation is always possible if you are brave and attentive enough. She very elegantly brought them all to life. Hanan breathes life into texts, stories, and theories. Most of all, she has constantly incited a capacity in me for wonder and an openness to surprise, to awe, to the endless potentialities of thought, imagination, and empathy. She is the one person I know who fully embodies what C. S. Lewis (1950) wrote one day: "But some day you will be old enough to start reading fairy tales again." She reads fairy tales and she trusts fairy tales; she reads them out loud to her students, inviting creatures of imaginative bodies to join us and speak to us words of truth and wisdom. She insisted on the attempt to restore the brilliance and inventiveness of little children, in how they pay attention to the world, how they express themselves wildly and freely. Dr. Hanan travels through time. Sometimes she's Alice, leading us into the perplexing, dazzling wonderland of epistemologies, philosophies. and concepts. Other times she stands at the back of class, or in a corner, quiet and observing, and patiently waits as we begin to stutter our ways to open up. Once we start talking with her, the conversation never ever really ends.

To Dr. Martina, who witnessed and very much contributed to the making of this manuscript, as well as to my overall experience at AUC. She guided me through my own thinking process, and introduced me to some of the most interesting and radical texts across several disciplines: social sciences, critical geographies, philosophy, urban studies. I would like to thank her for her astounding generosity, sharing every piece of knowledge she has with those who surround her; for always welcoming and encouraging new ideas; and for the diligent and continuous effort she makes as she "keeps her eyes open" for new ways of thinking and new modes of learning. I would like to thank her for bearing with me and helping me pass the emotional lows and intellectual blocks. She has given me precious and absolutely timeless advice on writing, how to make it happen and how to let it, simultaneously, unmake and remake her. Writing is life, she used to tell me, and it is from her that I learned that the flow of writing is the flow of life itself. One does not freeze life in order to write about it; they both happen together and to each other.

To Dr. Ian, whom I met in 2016. Together with Dr. Kiven Strohm, we ventured into the world of affect theory and different approaches to reading and writing, to theorizing, to doing ethnography, to living, thinking, and relating to one another. I would like to thank them for being genuinely open to exploring new territories of thought with me, and for constantly pushing me to write my heart out, without fear. In the last months of writing this manuscript, they were there as I went through many moments of uncertainty and doubt, fear, and anxiety. They always knew how it feels to be an MA student rushing after deadlines, and they kindly provided support, understanding, and very helpful insight from their own experiences with writing, so as to make the process easier and less lonesome.

To Dr. Munira, who blew my mind with her creativity, courage, and warmth of heart. She challenged me to look for life where there seems to be only violence, destruction, and death. I want to thank her for pushing me to pay attention to the silences and absences, and to look for what lies behind them. I remember we shared a passion for Elena Ferrante novels, and they allowed me to extend my imagination and further pursue that passion, describe it, question it, trace it, write about it. I will never forget the sound of their laughter.

To Dr. Dina, who very powerfully helped me ground myself in thinking about the everyday dynamics of and relations between work, personhood, and the different kind of labor it takes to "make" a living. I thank her for being extremely empathetic, patient, and supportive with me. I thank her for making Fall 2017, which was a difficult and intense semester to say the least, much more bearable and kind, and for pushing my research topic by generously and openly sharing every bit of academic knowledge as well as personal bits and stories about friendship that might help enhance and enrich my project.

To Dr. Ramy, who grounded me in the various views on and approaches to ethnography, ethnographic methods, and ways of doing fieldwork. I thank him for taking in my very first attempts and "baby trials" at doing interviews. He has given me the rooms of time and trust that enabled me to share those tests and tryouts with him and with the rest of my colleagues. I thank him and I will always cherish the space of learning and interacting that he has constructed and invited me into, with much comfort and great care.

To Hana El Gaby, to Lily Leach, to Sarah Zidan, to Noha Fikry, to Mariz Kelada, and to Suzan Tharwat, the beautiful, kind, enthusiastic, and strong women in my life who taught me a myriad of things about friendship. My life would have not been the same without them, and I cannot even imagine this study being a potentiality without all the love, encouragement, understanding, and acceptance they have given me. I look up to them, and they never cease to astound me. They are worlds of care and of compassion, and they are also manifestations of resilience and bravery, and it amazes me how they carry on with the difficulties of life (with me!) with relentless grace and absolute resilience. They tolerated and embraced me when I could not bear my own self, and I am grateful to them for making me who I am and for holding me so gently, allowing me to breathe and bloom. Their doors, ears, hearts were always open for me and I hope I have not failed them.

To Nadia, Yasmine, Mohamed El-Hadidi, Ahmed Serougi, Amro Ali, Hagar Adam, Sarah Bahgat, Nadiene Muhammed, I thank them for sharing their Alexandria(s) with me, for guiding me into their lives and their homes, for the very openness that made our experiences and back-and-forth trips profoundly rich and exciting. I thank them for showing me as many lives to the city of Alexandria as there could be; they have expanded my horizons beyond what I expected and ever imagined. We met either here, in Cairo, or there, in Alexandria, and sometimes we accompanied each other on the road between the two. It is impossible to think of Alexandria now without thinking of each one of them and the forceful and insightful stories they have shared with me, both personal and otherwise. Being in their company shattered any possible estrangement I had or could have had with the city that is not "my hometown," as their company enabled me to make a home out of it. And for that I shall be eternally grateful.

To Hussein el Hajj for the remarkable and dazzling talks we had, for sharing experiences of and ideas about friendship and cities, for giving me his time and sharing his stories, thoughts, and reflections. I thank him for the laughter and tears and the many pauses, stutters, and silences we shared. My fieldwork experience was anything but typical because of his intellectual openness and willingness to improvise with me as we constructed this work together.

To Haytham Wardani, Mohamed Anwar, and Robin Moger, my faraway friends whose voices perpetually reverberate in me.

To Hatem Salem and Mohammed Elmasry, I thank them for believing in me, for their constant efforts at being there for me. They have allowed me to share both my dreams and nightmares with them; they always listened and cared. Their wisdom echoes in me even when they are away. Whatever they have given me I keep and carry with me wherever I go. They have made possible a daydream I once had about friendship. In fact, the friendship they have made possible for me exceeds the one I had imagined in my dream in so many ways.

To Diana Magdy, Chehab Adel, Ahmed Abo Elfadl, Ahmed Abdelwahab, Salma Salah, Salma Wardani, Sherief Ahmed, Maged Nader, Muhammed el-Hajj, I thank them for the wonderful times of friendship, and the memories that we have and still make together.

To the friends with whom I occupied the AUC gardens, who taught me so much about myself: Alaa Ateyyah, Aly Alfy, Alya Marakby, Amyra Mahmoud, Doaa Kaddah, Ghosoun Tawfik, Hagar Adam, Heba ElSawy, Radwa Fouda, Mostafa Mohie, Noor Amin, Farida Hussein, Salma Khaira, I thank them for their brilliant humor, their intelligence, their curious spirits and lovely presence. Being a student again at twenty-eight would not have been nearly as exhilarating and terrific if it hadn't been for them.

To Nouran Fawzi and Tasneem Gad, the goddesses of Alexandria! Tasneem is the photographer behind the cover image.

To the Crillon hotel staff, who hosted my wandering self in Alexandria. To my cats, Poussi and Gucci. To Cairo's Downtown and Alexandria's Downtown, where I get lost and found and lost again.

To professor Iman Hamdy for her exceeding generosity and the tremendous help and support that she very kindly provided all throughout the journey of publishing this work.

To my brother and sister, my very first friends. And to my mother; I am still understanding her love, but it certainly is something like the moonlight, as Lola Ridge's poem "Mother" goes, that constantly turns harsh things to beauty. It cannot be described, but it keeps spreading miles and years ahead of me and beyond me. It is what keeps me alive.

Prelude

My friend,

I am writing to you because it is you who have been haunting me, accompanying me, tagging along, and muddling through the days with me. Following me, calling me to follow you. I'm writing to you because there is so much to who you are, how you came up to me, and how your presence happened to disorganize my life, opening me to move beyond myself. "'I didn't think it would turn out this way' is the secret epitaph of intimacy," says Lauren Berlant (1998). I didn't think, I still don't think, I'll ever understand that which is enigmatic, holy, almost instinctive that draws me to you. But to exoticize, romanticize, or idolize you or us would be to take away from the brilliance of the flawed, inconsistent, imperfect, and fluid nature of our relationship—it would be to ruin it and kill you and that's not what I have intended to do.

What I have tried my best to do is to understand the promise(s) that our friendship holds and perhaps the threats as well. The tenderness, the violence, and what lies between, which is most of the time a push and pull between both. I am writing this to you because you are distant enough for a conversation but close enough to see me, listen to me, and understand. After all, I believe friendship is precisely this promise, the promise that there will be a cushion when you take the leap, that you will be heard, seen, understood, borne with in a relation of mutual reciprocity, "taking each other on and in but never collapsing the distance that allows for attention" (Berlant 2016: 406).

In writing this manuscript I have spoken to, walked with, and lived among friends, I have learned about and from them, I have listened to what they said and tried my best to pay attention to all that which insists on lurking in silence, dwelling comfortably in this enabling and generous space of intimacy that lets whatever wants to be, be. We spoke of the difficulty of passing the days in a precarity that feels as if one had been swallowed by a whale, and in the darkness of the whale's belly we need to find ways to figure out how best to carry on, together. We spoke of our home cities and together improvised our ways to reconstruct our cities as our homes and our homes as still belonging to those cities, Cairo and Alexandria; we had to constantly reshuffle and remake our maps, our ways home, our daily routes as they insanely alter, shift, disappear, reappear, and become otherwise—different street names, torn-down buildings, new bridges, abandoned theaters, burnt police stations, central squares becoming car garages, histories erased and others made up. We spoke of ourselves and one another, how as friends we are deep and strange reservoirs of knowledge, of accumulations and memories, embarrassments, disappointments, dreams, revelations and traces of the other, that are as valuable, precious, and rare as they are dangerous, sometimes profound, shocking, and overwhelming.

My research had to be an episode of life, a long conversation. Conversations, as Tim Ingold recently argued, have three important and distinguishing properties: 1. They are processes; they carry on. 2. They are open-ended, not aimed at a final conclusion, but rather at posing more questions and engendering further life. 3. They are dialogical; they go on between and among people. This is precisely why I crafted my manuscript in the form of a dialogic correspondence, an assemblage of voices that speak to one another, sometimes complement, other times problematize and challenge one another. My insistence on pursuing the topic of friendship, with all the complexities this entails, stems from my belief that knowledge is something that emerges continually in between humans, non-humans, objects, and materialities, atmospheres, amidst tensions and frictions, confusions and attractions, attachments, promising beginnings and world-shattering ends. It is difficult to come to terms with the fact that I had to wrap up this conversation and perhaps even add a "conclusion" section at the end, because I think the term "conclusion," meaning final judgment, verdict, or reasoning, reflects a sense of finitude and finishedness. It will not by any means be able to serve, enhance, or enrich the arguments I have tried to closely engage with—precisely the open-endedness that is characteristic of the relationship of friendship. To conclude a friendship, in my opinion, is to terminate it, and perhaps it is in this space here and now that I can try to add what might constitute a meaningful end note to my manuscript, a study that started by grounding itself in the radical possibilities of friendship. It must also be acknowledged that the possibilities are not always radical, and that sometimes, the possibilities of becoming friends lie in the impossibility of being friends.

Let me elaborate on that point further. In a time characterized by anxiety, stress, disappointment, precarity, existential threats of climate change, extreme experiences of capitalist inequalities and political uncertainty, people's ideas and fantasies around what constitutes a good life have also significantly taken a different turn. Good-life fantasies, imaginations around how our lives might "add up to something"— for example, the fantasy of enduring reciprocity in couples, families, political institutions, markets, and so one—have certainly been put on edge, strained, dwindled, withered, frayed. To be more clear, this is not to say that this hiccup or glitch in the reproduction of life, or this situation of crisis, is exceptional to history in any way, but I'm trying to see how it can be traced as a mediated affect, embedded and entrenched in the everyday, a thing sensed, lived, and shared. It is experienced in transactions and transitions, unfolding in stories about navigating what is overwhelming and finding and maintaining one's footing in new manners of being, to keep bearing within a thick present. In this moment of un-foreclosed experience, our open, contingent, and precarious ways of living require a tremendous labor of constant reimagining and readjusting in order to stay afloat.

In this mess, the complexity of being bound to life, being held in place, having an anchor feeling-at-home in the world becomes interrupted, and in this perpetual state of suspension we linger, in proximity to each other, constantly becoming lost together. I am a part of that hum that resonates around me, the everyday individual as well as collective attempts to hold on to something that makes life bearable as it presents itself ambivalently, incoherently. My project stems from that fact that I wanted to be able to capture something that happens in the middle of those attempts, in the atmospheres of sociality, in moments of expressive and emancipative relatedness as well as awkward silences, neither precisely euphoria nor despair, but the emergence of intimacy as a potential footing in the world, while not knowing exactly how and whether this scene of collaboration and companionship will unfold, where it will wind up, or what potentials it might open up. Throughout my fieldwork, I dwelled in friendship, I took residence in it. It sometimes seemed like a home to which I can return, other times more like a sailing ship, constantly moving as some people hop on and others jump off. It sometimes held me and at other times failed me. Friendship comes with knotty entailments: we make mistakes, we disappoint each other, we abandon each other, we mean no harm but accidents happen. The hazy luminosity of the promise of friendship would shimmer on some days and dim on others. I wanted to be able to write an ethnography together and collaboratively with you, without having to draw contours between us in order to define you or myself. I wanted this ethnography to capture your voice and mine in polyphony, an assemblage of moments and encounters of harmony and dissonance in which our autonomous melodies (voices) can intertwine. I wanted to have a long, slow, open-ended conversation with you, not free of humor, wonder, surprise. We couldn't (perhaps we never wanted to) define friendship, but it came and went, embodied in moments of joy and sometimes of confusion. My ethnographic journey started in the middle of friendship and moved from there—tracing the multiple rhythms and crises that shape the immediacy of intimacy in relation to broader political and structural durations. Those series of rhythms, patterns, habits, collaborative acts of living (eating, smoking, talking, working, walking, complaining) together were in themselves astoundingly rich and profound, in the knowledges they encapsulate and in how they articulate, convey, and express various modes of creativity, inventiveness, human capacities for care, adjustment, carrying on, and living with one another.

Friendship emerged as a possibility of living in proximity to a dear other, and not being crushed by what brings us together. Living with friendship is not the same as living under it. Friendship is not a proof or a contract of unending belonging and integration; it is not about a promise of being happy and fulfilled. Neither is it about accepting, containing, and bearing another for good. It is neither a project of forever-ness nor of any guaranteed positive outcomes. Friendship involves many other things than holding hands and leaning, crying on the friend's shoulder, relying on the constance and continuity of the friend's presence. If a three-year training in anthropology offered me anything, it is an awareness of the complex and multilayered nature of things no matter how much they seem to be known, finished, understood, fully grasped. Look more closely: it is only something that hasn't been looked at long enough and given sufficient time and attention. Like most precious things, friendship is for the most part overwhelming and difficult, almost impossible to explain, and sometimes almost impossible to keep. The radical possibilities of friendship indeed include the possibility of its death, which is a part of the paradox of becoming, becoming ourselves/friends/ourselves/otherwise. Friendship, again, is both the home and the ship that admits to movement as both its condition and its consequence. How we throw ourselves actively into this relationship of becoming is not metaphorical or philosophical but depends on actual labor of the individual(s), acts of giving and acts of receiving, witnessing, catching up, staying in touch, attentiveness, responsiveness, and response-ability that render lives answerable to one another. Friendships have vague beginnings and even vaguer futures, and I believe that friendship can only be understood in the complex and open-ended paradox of becoming, as something that is constantly moved toward but never really reached, never fully fathomed, never fully realized. Yet it remains life's difficult task to answer the question of how and whether friendship abides, and to understand that it can only be traced by following the horizon of life as it moves—for example, the moment when a friend rests on the other's shoulder in the metro and feels safe enough to fall asleep, right there and right then.

CHAPTER 1

Introduction

In this research, I would like to explore the notion of friendship in contemporary Egypt, as a contingent relationship born and maintained among various conditions of political, economic, and urban precarity and uncertainty. Particularly, I'm interested in looking at the affective and creative modes of attachment, relating, and belonging that people constantly invent and experiment with, when life is too messy for categories to hold. By tracing and accompanying friends and networks of friendship emerging in and across the two biggest cities of Egypt, Cairo and Alexandria, my goal is to co-construct an ethnography about the contemporary meanings, forms, and purposes of friendship among young Egyptians. The main question running throughout this work is: What can the relationships of friendship do? My aim is to provide a rich ethnographic contribution to the existing anthropological literature on Egypt, by focusing on intimacy, coexistence, and companionship.

This ethnography is founded on multiple co-constitutive conversations—virtual, theoretical, and abstract, on one hand, and real and bodily, on another. The aim is to renew and revive the question of "What can friendships do?" (Foucault quoted in Rainbow 1997:138), while letting this textual space serve as a window for possible answers and articulations. From various encounters and talks with friends, a particular portrait of friendship, its meaningful presence or rather absence, emerged as a possibility of gathering "around" something yet not "under" it, a co-constitutive entanglement, a relationship that at best does not aim to crush, constrain, or fix the roles of the subjects involved.

1

This perhaps could be read as a line of continuity from the many lines inspired by Foucault's question "What could be played?" (Foucault quoted in Rainbow 1997:140). Yet I would like to repeat over and over the term "possibility" and stretch it to admit also the impossibilities and the limits of friendship. I imagine the possibility as the dots between and... and... and (Deleuze and Guattari 2004:27), which is precisely the open-endedness that wants to free itself from predetermined before(s) and after(s). This is not to say that friendship does not seek consistency or does not involve dreams of futures of togetherness and safe, ideal, and steady lifelong relations of companionship. Yet there is a lot to be said about ideas and imaginations of the "future" when one does not have much luxury to maintain a slot in the present. It is precisely the acute presence of conditions of precarity (political, economic, social, infrastructural) that drives the myriad creative and radical negotiations, navigations, and variations of subjects on "how/where to go next?" The questions that my research attempts to open up are rather focused on the "affective" negotiations, in other words reworkings, reconfigurations, and remakings of notions and practices of relations, socialities, and intimacies between friends.

Inheritances, Traces, and Trails of Intimacy

Friends constantly move around and with us, tell us things, challenge, accompany, confuse, lift, disappoint, and ground us. In trying to think about the bond of friendship, one of the primary conditions would be to situate oneself not "in place" but "along paths" of correspondence. By that I mean that friendship is precisely born and maintained in the very entwining of the ever-moving trajectories and processes of becoming. It emerges always "in the middle" and "in-between" things, where the friend embodies the condition for my "passing from one world to another" (Deleuze and Guattari 1994:18). To trace the bond of friendship in textual literature is to actively surf among and with thinkers, philosophers, cultural theorists, artists, writers, and social scientists in a sea of shifting waves. Coming and going, those waves of thought and experience "travel in circuits of impact and reaction" (Stewart 2017:197) whereby the authors speak to each other and to us about something that keeps slipping in and out of existence, hardly completely graspable or fully fathomable.

This is not to say that friendship in and of itself comprises elements of mystification or perplexity, but rather that what friendship stands for, how it is represented, established, perceived, and maintained, varies tremendously from one context, time, and place to another. In order to trace friendship in literature one needs to cultivate a sincere "openness to a world-in-formation" (Ingold 2011:69), a world that constantly becomes other than what it was the moment that the figure of the "friend" walks in or out. With this in mind, the tracing of friendship in different academic (and non-academic) genres and texts has been an intimate, animated, and unfolding process that must be traced slowly and with profound care. Rather than trying to formulate clear-cut definitions of friendship, I sought to assemble an array of voices, narratives, theories, and reflections from within the crack—the gap or the distance (in time as well as in space) between the different collaborators and interlocutors, the real and the virtual, the ones I have met, the ones I have only encountered in texts and in others' stories—that will allow more complex, layered, and comprehensive understandings of friendship to emerge.

Fragmented philosophies on friendship. The dialogues of Plato and Cicero, the monographs of Aristotle, the letters of Seneca, the essays of Montaigne and Kierkegaard, along with the textual contributions of other prominent Greek and Roman philosophers, have founded the quintessential philosophical legacy on friendship, the very crucial labor of engaging, drawing on, and variously articulating the core values and nuances at play in this complex and multilayered interpersonal bond. However fertile the ground that these bases of thought have established, the messy muddling of human beings seems to have constantly exceeded, rather than merely mirrored, the systematic neatness of categories and dynamics of social reciprocities. For example, in *Friendship: A Philosophical Reader* (1993), the editor Neera Kapur Badhwar compiles a selection of essays by fifteen contemporary scholars in philosophy who present a diverse range of in-depth examinations of historical philosophical speculations on friendship, drawing on, for example, Aristotle and Kant. While one can certainly think with and through as well as benefit from Aristotle's famous classification of types of friendship,[1] this research stems from frustration caused by the inability of philosophical abstractions to match

---

1   Based on (a) utility, (b) pleasure, and/or (c) goodness and virtue.

the messy dynamism of life and the wide spectrum of interpersonal relationships. What I hope to contribute with this anthropological study is a material, imperfect, fluid (and I hear Eve Sedgwick's voice adding: "weak") theory of the unpredictability and ungraspability of the affective and social bonds between human beings. Weak theory (Sedgwick 1997) is a mode of theorizing that consists of slow and attentive tracing of the "generative modalities of impulses, daydreams, ways of relating, distractions, strategies, failures, encounters, and worldings of all kinds" (Stewart 2008:73). It inhabits the space of attending to things so as to constantly be able to track the possible throwing-together of things, and the open question of "where they might go." It does not aim to judge the value of analytic objects or imprison the analytic subject; rather, it tracks the potential modes of knowing and relating that are present in and between the objects and subjects in moments where things throw themselves together. In other words, "weak" theory is a way of attending to life as a problem and an open question, not a simple and unified repository of systematic and structural effects, but rather an ever-shifting composition of actualities and potentialities, contact zones and structures of feeling (Williams 1977), residues of moments of watching and waiting, as together people "make something of things" (Stewart 2011:447).

The writing of this manuscript is laced with loss, awe, and *imponderabilia*,[2] particularly because thinking of friends launches one on a journey that inevitably stretches over one's entire life. The journey runs from childhood to teenage years to adulthood, passing through early daydreams and nightmares, holidays on the beach, terribly long school mornings, juvenile adrenaline rushes and forceful stirrings, first-time experiences, realizations, confusions, the agonizing embarrassment of early disappointments, and the aching naiveté of the young heart and self. Everything seemed either life-shattering or world-building, no in-betweens. How and how much one anchors oneself in friendship is a

---

2 In producing his theory of Participant Observation (key to anthropological methodology and inquiry), the pioneering anthropologist Bronislaw Malinowski (1922) used "imponderabilia" to refer to routines, gestures, expressions, actions, and things that are not often explained or made elaborate in the everyday language. Therefore, they require devoted attention by the ethnographer rather than any automated form of reporting. In other words, imponderabilia are things not easily translated into and not commonly articulated through the use of normative and systematic modes of speech and expression.

matter that varies from one life to another, depending on one's circumstances. Yet the knowledge, influences, and impressions one acquires from and with friends at different stages in life invariably occupy a central position in one's fundamental conceptions of the self, the other, and the wide world one inhabits.

Surfing the waves of friendship in thought.

> *We must give up trying to know those to whom we are linked by something essential; by this I mean we must greet them in the relation with the unknown in which they greet us as well, in our estrangement. Friendship, this relation without dependence, without episode, yet into which all of the simplicity of life enters, passes by way of the recognition of the common strangeness that does not allow us to speak of our friends but only to speak to them, not to make of them a topic of conversations (or essays), but the movement of understanding in which, speaking to us, they reserve, even on the most familiar terms, an infinite distance, the fundamental separation on the basis of which what separates becomes relation.* (Blanchot 1997:290–291)

To "surf" is to ride a wave toward and along the shore but never really reach the shoreline. It is a movement of a body over a moving wave that demands vigilant sensory alertness, physical stamina and fortitude, mindful attention, and an openness to letting yourself be carried. In a recent magazine interview, Arundhati Roy, one of my favorite novelists and certainly one of India's most prominent writers and political activists, poignantly described the friendships in her life as resembling "walking on lily pads" (Roy 2017a). I found that description astounding, because lily pads are very fine, round leaves that float ever-so-delicately over the surface of water. I have never done the water sport of surfing, but I can stare into pictures of water lilies, and video footage of real surfers, for hours on end. Roy's comment has immensely inspired me, in a metaphorical sense, to think in the same manner and try to float over the waves of friendships-in-thought as well as real-life friendships between thinkers. The real-life friendships, connections, and collaborations between thinkers, the collisions between their ways of thinking and theorizing, I believe have immensely influenced my interest in this relationship and what it can offer, in the immediacy of the everyday but also on the epistemological, conceptual, and theoretical levels. I believe it is necessary in my ethnographic endeavor to start with exhibiting and thinking through at least a few examples of friendships that occurred between thinkers who were, in a sense, to borrow Avner Segall's term, "constant companions" (2001:584). The act of tracing of the theme of friendship that lies at the heart of this study does not follow a "unidirectional" route that begins with the field and ends in academe, or vice versa. It is instead a broadening and a stretching of a conversation, in which "voices in the field"—who are in this case the real-life friends—and "voices from the field"—the academic/virtual interlocutors—speak to, challenge, disturb, and sometimes problematize each other. The two realms never were, are not, and will hardly ever be separable; instead "they are constantly and simultaneously implicated with/by one another" (Segall 2001:583). I am imagining a number of people gathering together to sit and have a conversation, in a lounge, a garden, a room, or an empty space, and I am drawn to an image where they arrange themselves in the form of a circle; they would not sit in rows.

Maurice Blanchot, the French writer, philosopher, and literary theorist, has been one immensely influential friend in the thought-process of this study. His writings accompanied me and engendered a certain "movement in understanding" across the temporal and spatial gaps between us. He died in 2003 and I read him in 2016. With Blanchot I imagined a conversation about the "infinite distance" and the "fundamental separation" between two friends, which according to him, is necessary to allow a speaking "to" and not "of" friends. There is a potential buried in the reciprocal estrangement between two friends, or so Blanchot taught me.

Friendship, with its fleeting qualities, holds a unique and consistently precious place in the works of Blanchot. His book *Friendship* (1997) is composed of 29 literary, cultural, and philosophical essays that read as a relation, a reflection, and a response to a community of writers including Georges Bataille, Franz Kafka, Lévi-Strauss, and others, while also producing a narrative of its own on themes such as literature, war, and translation. The authors are brought together in this book, and in their togetherness, the rhythm and the life of the text is created, especially by

Georges Bataille, who was one of Blanchot's closest friends and whose spirit haunts Blanchot's words in direct and indirect ways. Blanchot performs friendship in his writing, such that the essays are not a series of diary entries, meditations, or confessions, but instead create relations and binding chains of thought with authors alive or dead, near or far, as well as with the ideas in their texts. In Blanchot's view, friendship survives the death, disappearance, or distance that separates those who identify as friends, in the very act of continuing the conversation. He writes in *The Unavowable Community*: "And it is in life itself that that absence of someone else has to be met. It is with that absence—its uncanny presence, always under the prior threat of a disappearance— that friendship is brought into play and lost at each moment, a relation without relation" (1988:25). The distance between two people—that is, the impossibility of complete understanding and communication— opens up an infinite possibility of new creations of meaning. By that I mean that this imponderable, mysterious, and vague element of friendship is somehow like a secret that unfolds in the making of the relationship itself. The unpredictability of this potential bonding takes the shape of an openness in thought, whereby the thought of the friend opens itself to us only in relation to "the strangeness of the end." Blanchot calls this "the interruption of being" that "brings us together in the difference and sometimes the silence of speech" (1997:291).

Besides his famous and compelling friendships with Georges Bataille and Emanuel Levinas, Blanchot maintained a deep friendship, a personal as well as a philosophical dialogue running throughout his life, with other figures like Jacques Derrida, Michel Foucault, and Dionys Mascolo. Mascolo was a French writer and political activist with whom Blanchot shares powerful memories of comradeship and flashes of a deep friendship (he insists on a distinction between the two terms) throughout decades of protesting/marching/writing against fascism, imperialism, and colonialism in the 1940s, 1950s, and 1960s. I learned about Mascolo first and primarily as a friend of Blanchot while reading Blanchot's article *For Friendship* (2000). The article reads like a beautiful montage or mise-en-scène of memoirs of various scenes of contact and disaster, demonstrations, disagreements, and friendships as "an effusiveness of heart and mind" (2000:26). Blanchot does not give the reader actual dates or a precise chronology of the events he narrates, stating that he always felt "ill-at-ease with any supposedly historical narrative," since whatever is constructed as truth is somehow also always "a deceptive reconstitution reliant on the arbitrary nature of remembering and forgetting" (Blanchot 2000:28). In the article he chronicles and contextualizes the beginning of his friendship with Mascolo, but at a later point he insists that the moment of birth of their bond actually came later. The experience of friendship, as Blanchot describes it, disrupts the typical scenario about instant clicking, and rather demonstrates a bond forming slowly over a series of encounters that flows over a period of time.

Between April and October 1988, Dionys Mascolo and Gilles Deleuze conducted a compelling written correspondence on the concept of friendship, published in the edited volume *Two Regimes of Madness: Texts and Interviews 1975–1995* in 2006. Deleuze initiated the conversation mainly to express his appreciation of and inspiration by Mascolo's work, *On an Effort of Memory*. He wrote to Mascolo that he could sense a certain kind of "secret" in the purity of his writings, and he ends his letter with the following gesture, which seems to me to transcend the boundaries of mere intellectual affinity: "Let me express my admiration, and, if you accept it, my friendship" (Deleuze 2006:327). A week later, and only a day after he received the letter, Mascolo replied, expressing not only gratitude but also surprise at having been "found out." Mascolo reflects on the idea of the secret in his writing and puts forward a proposition that perhaps this particular kind of secret—one that does not seek refuge in shame or humor, a secret without secrets, a secret that does not seek to kindle or provoke other secrets—if recognized by another person can become a sufficient basis for "any possible friendship" (2006:328).

This correspondence is in itself a beginning of friendship. At the same time, it gives us a space to examine and reflect upon the broader concept of friendship. It reveals friendship as both an embodiment and an articulation of a thought that originally resides within the contours of the self, yet one that is also always excessive, always moving, and constantly seeking a space of co-habitation where it can grow and become. Perhaps Mascolo's conception of friendship is premised on a common language, or more precisely a common pre-language. "Friendship comes first" somehow, as an affective space of mutual relativity. This understanding of friendship gives room to the unrevealed and the unspoken to be and become of significance, without need of the spoken word as evidence of intimacy. Closeness is not measured only by the shared, but also by what dwells in silence, in distress, in tormenting uncertainty, in utter unfinished-ness or incompleteness inside each person, and longs for the company of another "distrusted" thought in the other.

After three months Deleuze writes back, taking the secret one step further, elaborating by rearticulating to Mascolo, and most probably to himself, that the idea of the possible friendship that is beginning to formulate is one that is based on a mutual "concern." Yet taking another step and moving deeper, Deleuze attempts to scrutinize and question the position of this "concern": whether friendship acts as the internal necessary condition for thought. In other words, does friendship come first? Deleuze is somehow inclined toward this supposition, which is an understanding that materializes, or becomes revealed, in his immensely rich, interesting, and generative friendship with Félix Guattari.

Gilles Deleuze's friendship with the French philosopher and psychoanalyst Félix Guattari began in the late 1960s, and through a series of significant intellectual collaborations, an active Ping-Pong of ideas between them over the years, they produced groundbreaking works such as *Anti-Oedipus* in 1972, *A Thousand Plateaus* in 1980, and in 1994 yet another milestone in their oeuvre, *What Is Philosophy*. Their works continue to be read internationally, inside academia as well as outside, long after the death of the two authors. There still seems to exist a curious and genuine interest among their readers in learning more about the ways in which this duo worked and produced their texts together, in and through friendship (see, for example, Dosse 2010). Since it is their own voices that concern us most, I have made a particular effort to collect, from the available sources, evidence of how they themselves viewed and described their collaboration. In *Two Regimes of Madness*, in the chapter "Letter to Uno: How Felix and I Worked Together," Deleuze wrote a simple and poetic note (originally to Kuniichi Uno, the Japanese translator of Deleuze, and a former student who later became a friend) on how peculiar his relationship with Guattari really was. While Deleuze compares Felix to the sea, "always seems to be in motion, sparkling with light," he then compares himself in an almost antonymic manner to a hill: "I don't move much . . . and the few movements I do have are internal" (2006:237). They were two very different people and had very different lives, yet in Deleuze's view their differences worked far more in their favor than against.

> *Gradually, a concept would acquire an autonomous existence, which sometimes we continued to understand differently. Working together was never a homogenization, but a proliferation, an accumulation of bifurcations, a rhizome ... Felix had these brainstorms, and I was like a lighting rod.* (Deleuze 2006:239)

Their first book was written primarily by means of an exchange of letters, and their personal meetings were irregular. In describing their work process for *Anti-Oedipus*, Guattari remarks: "At the outset, it was less a matter of sharing a common understanding than sharing the sum of our uncertainties" (Guattari quoted in Dosse 2010:8).

Similarly, Deleuze remarked that the collaboration between their minds and the possibility of creation of thought fundamentally involved "stuttering ellipses" and "inarticulate sounds" (Deleuze quoted in Dosse 2010:9), and that along the invisible and imperceptible "line of flight or of a flow" between both of their minds "things come to pass, becomings evolve, revolutions take shape" (Deleuze quoted in Dosse 2010:10). The shared concept that emerges and formulates in the "and" is an outcome or a culmination of a profound intimacy in thought, but not a collision. It remains a potentiality that belongs to both, and a property of neither (Roach 2012). As a project of life, friendship here bears "the imprint of a historical relationship yet points toward a posthumous political project with a life of its own" (Roach 2012:2). This explanation highlights the potentialities of friendship, beyond merely tracing its conceptual terrain.

In Michel Foucault's voice I hear a call to friendship as a way of revolutionizing the possibility of human relations and transformative capacities. Foucault's theory of friendship becomes more visible in his late writings on notions of self-care as activism and as a mode of resistance. To him, friendship can be a way of life (Foucault quoted in Rainbow 1997:138) that disturbs the hierarchal and normative structures of identity and subjectivity. As a radical and anti-institutional act, Foucault offers a view of friendship as in and of itself a political fabric capable of engendering new conceptions of union and community bonds, beyond and against the institutionalized, calcified, and worn-out categories of legitimization and the constraining agendas of belonging and identity politics. Borrowing its title from an interview with Foucault in the 1980s, *Friendship as a Way of Life* by Tom Roach (2012) deeply engages with Foucault's "spare but suggestive" (Roach 2012:12) philosophical speculations, conceptual advancements, and politically oriented arguments on the relationship of friendship, as well as accounts of his real-life friendships (in particular Foucault's interesting and complex friendship with the French writer and photographer Hervé Guibert). By introducing and emphasizing the relevance of "betrayal" to the mutual theory of friendship between Foucault and Guibert, Roach ended up with an unusual and compelling account of friendship that powerfully disrupts the idealized and canonical philosophies of friendship from Aristotle through Carl Schmitt. "Foucault's concept of friendship is anything but utopian," writes Roach, "betrayal, distance, brutal honesty, indeed, an impersonal intimacy founded in estrangement are its makings" (Roach 2012:8–9). By delving into the minutiae of details that constituted the Guibertian–Foucaultian relationship, Roach finds supports for an argument (inspired by Foucault) where the most unorthodox and troubling aspects of friendship become its very foundation.

At the heart of Roach's book lies an attempt to identify the key elements of the Foucaultian discourse on friendship as a radical form of gathering that resists representation, eludes categorical and structural definitions, and refuses to consolidate into a singular identity. In the distance between two friends resides a perpetual foreignness and irreducibility, a politics of shared estrangement that is always open to the infinite variation of being, whereby, as Roach argues, "its very unrepresentability points toward a politics beyond representation" (Roach 2012:149). Roach draws on Foucault's literature as well as his personal life in order to sense the fleeting visions of the nature of friendship that Foucault grappled with. At the same time, Roach's work can be seen as a part of a larger project aimed at imagining broader and more radical modes of relationality and sociality. Like Deleuze, Foucault sees friendship as a way of being and becoming, and friends as "those with whom we work on the historical conditions of our existence, and those with whom we share the practice of becoming who we are" (Webb 2003:119).

It might be useful to pause momentarily to reflect on the conversation that has been taking place in the past few pages. I hear Jacques Derrida's voice, then the voice of another, but I am in a bit of a haze. I am already embedded in this assemblage of voices. Yet those acts of telling, as Michael Taussig would suggest, are like rites of passage that get stuck in transmission; they remain hanging, suspended. I imagine Taussig standing up, looking quite bewitched, mesmerized, haunted by a metaphor. "Like throwing a stone across a pond and see how it skips,"[3] he finally says, waving his hand as if tossing a pebble across water and watching how and how far it bounces off the surface.

One must be careful not to fall into the trap of conceptualizing friendship as a universal category, the grammar of which is constructed and validated by a Eurocentric mode of thought. The rich genealogies of friendship can be traced to different regions in the world, as well as different historical instances and contingencies, diverse epistemologies, understandings and practices that are all equally foundational to cultural, social, and knowledge production and transference. It is crucial to examine the various accounts and interpretations of friendship. They are not mere "traveling concepts" but lifeworlds carrying values and wisdoms of their own.

João Biehl (2013:584) poses an abrupt question: "So do we need philosophy to reflect on our fieldwork?" I share Biehl's view that there is a point to be made about the interaction between philosophy and anthropology as a creative exchange that should rest primarily on the unfolding ethnographic present "in all its repetitions, singularities and ambiguities" (Biehl and Locke 2017:113). Rather than emanating from concept, this mode of doing philosophy emanates from lifeworlds. In the edited volume *The Ground Between: Anthropologists Engage Philosophy* (Das et al. 2014), a number of eminent anthropologists such as Arthur Kleinman, Michael Jackson, Veena Das, Ghassan Hage, and João Biehl (among others) manage to cleverly and persuasively tread the "ground between" anthropology and philosophy by initiating an open

---

3   I had the pleasure and the honor of attenting the Ethnographic Writing Workshop given by Professor Michael Taussig in Cairo on 18 April 2018. The workshop was held by the School of Humanities & Social Sciences (HUSS) at AUC New Cairo, where Professor Taussig wove theory with fieldwork and beautifully narrated ideas, thoughts, questions and reflections on storytelling, ethnographic thinking, making and doing. I have quoted this sentence from his talk.

encounter with particular philosophical conceptual renderings of the world, of social relationships, and of everyday phenomena. The authors approach and confront 'P'hilosophy courageously yet with great care, in a genuine attempt to challenge its taken-for-granted epistemological authority and question the legitimacy of the accepted hierarchy of knowledge(s) between Western philosophical modes of theorizing and the less regarded "other" modalities of doing and using philosophy. To Biehl, "people must come first in our work" (Biehl 2013:587); if philosophers tell stories with concepts, then anthropologists can and should be able to tell stories with "instances of human becomings" (Biehl 2014:115). The irreducibility, plurality, and contingency of ways of being, becoming, and relating can provide the possibility of alternative, exciting, and viable pathways to knowledge and wisdom. Ideas, in that sense, emerge within the interstices between the complex and multilayered landscapes of "life bricolage" (Biehl 2013:584), the creative, relational, and constantly utilized capacities of human beings to improvise, to live, to think, to adapt. In Biehl's terms, this bricolage is "what people make, often agonizingly, out of whatever is available to them to endure, understand, and desire against all odds" (2013:584). In the end, the people, the social worlds they create and inhabit, and the conditions they manage (or not) to cope with are always more muddled, messy, and "unfinished" than philosophical ideals tend to describe. Bit by bit, the philosophical conversation turns to explore and illuminate the anthropological efforts to study friendship.

I love the idea that a work can float a concept, allowing the spirit of play to enter the fraught space of curiosity, scholarship, curation, synthesis, explanation, desperation, aggression, and desire that engaged criticality amounts to. Without play, nothing moves, as we know from losing teeth. When Bergson writes that laughter is "a momentary anesthesia of the heart," this is what he gestures toward . . . . The sheer impact of a thing induces a suspension of self-encounter where breathing, noticing, and not knowing happen so that an alien concept or world can begin to be metabolized, to become different and intimate. (Berlant 2015:274)

Anthropology and the study of friendship. Generally, friendship has occupied a marginal position within the sociological and anthropological scholarship and literature, whereas kinship has been made to "encom-pass the entire field of sociality" (Santos-Granero, as cited in Bunnell et al. 2012:9). Its dynamics, characteristics, and potentialities tend to be subsumed under broader social categories like "community," "kin," and "networks." We usually come across the term "friend" in the acknowl-edgments or the preface of a publication, but it is very rare that the conceptualization of friendship occupies the heart of the work, the main center of analytic attention. Especially in the case of a region like the Middle East, the ways in which it is "worlded" and "attended to" in contemporary anthropological writings reflect a certain preoccupation with the broad question of defining the social "order," "entity," or "struc-ture" that would in turn produce explanations of the activities of the actors within, that other domains (such as politics, economics, or psy-chology) might have failed to fully capture or make sense of. As Bruno Latour argues, it is as if "the social could explain the social" (2005:160), whereby the kinds of questions tackled and the topics pursued offer a rigid outlook on what the ingredients of "society" are or could be. Society, according to this approach, acts as an already-out-there place-holder in which all actors live, interact, assemble, and disassemble. Yet this approach to the "social" as a finished category greatly hinders the knowledge production process, as it reduces the human actors to a range of mere informants that represent and at best reproduce the larger con-text in which they are situated and "of which they see only a tiny part" (Latour 2005:32).

If this problem can be considered one of methodology, then the question of friendship's position in the literature, among other forms of social relations, remains unresolved. Another suggestive point may be, as Michael Eve proposes in *Is Friendship a Sociological Topic?* (2002), that friendship does not hold a "structural" significance in the sociological "paradigm" of the typical "social unit" within modern society. Eve elaborates that the perception of friendship in mod-ern sociological endeavors confines it to the realm of the "private," often interpreted as a "free-floating dyadic relationship" between two individuals, and hence representing only the "personal" traits of the persons in question rather than webs embedded in a larger social world (Eve 2002:387). By situating friendship in the realm of the pri-vate, the individualistic, as if it can be detached from the surrounding economic, political, and cultural conditions, it is removed from the workings of the larger social, political, and economic sphere and hence cannot offer the significant insights that closer and more grounded investigations of friendship might provide. In this view, friendships, as informal and non-contractual bonds, have "no clear normative status" and thus can only be defined by the active, ongoing, reciprocal work that is necessary to sustain them. Eve describes this as problematic because it casts friendship as highly affective, porous, and difficult to grasp "scientifically." When researchers insist on polarizing friendship as either a highly emotional, individualistic, and personal one-to-one relation, or groups of people glued together socially by a particular set of systematic or instrumental conditions (like neighborhood or community), the relationship of friendship becomes rather obscured, and is pushed, for the sake of analysis, into one or another form of sociality that acts as a means to other ends.

To take the conversation forward, I will devote this section to exploring and engaging with some of the major attempts by social scientists during the last decade to focus solely on the theme of friendship. I have chosen the works mainly on the basis of their substantial contribution of ethnographic accounts, sharp anthropological analyses, and focused discussions. *The Anthropology of Friendship* (1999) edited by Sandra Bell and Simon Coleman, offers an excellent comparative study of friendship in different geopolitical contexts. The editors assemble a valuable selection of ethnographic case studies drawn from contemporary Europe, East Africa, Brazil, and China, as well as ancient Ireland. The book proposes a useful critical approach that questions the applicability of Western, Eurocentric notions of friendship and intimacy in other contexts. Not only does it examine how friendship is configured in geographic worlds outside of the "West," but it goes more deeply to dispute the assumption that "friendship" has an essential definition and shape that can be applied everywhere and at all times. Through their different ethnographic lenses, the various authors consider "whether it makes sense to think of friendship as existing in mutually comprehensible ways across cultures" (Bell and Coleman 1999:2). They identify and question a number of rigid and seemingly universal, but mainly Western, assumptions about friendship, allowing their ethnographic material to challenge their universal validity. For example, in Mario Aguilar's insightful chapter on pastoral societies in East Africa, he argues for an understanding of friendship as a "social and human process, culturally and contextually constructed" (Bell and Coleman 1999:170) that inevitably takes different forms in different societies. In assessing friendships within pastoral societies, he argues that its manifestations grow out of "localized ways of being human and of being social" (171). The social importance of friendship here does not lie in its situatedness, either before or after that of kinship relations, but each of these categories continuously bleeds into, shapes, and is shaped by the other. This particular outlook blurs the sharp distinction that is made in many anthropological and sociological works between friendship and kinship. Those works mainly seek to draw definitive lines around friendship in order to signify specific notions related to autonomy, voluntarism, and freedom—in other words, friendship as a willed and agential act. While it is important to acknowledge the differences between formal kinship structures and friendship ties, kinship and friendship should be treated as "partially overlapping rather than mutually exclusive, classificatory terms" (Herman 1987:19, as cited in Bell and Coleman 1999:7).

Another ethnography in the same volume, conducted by Deborah Reed-Danahay in the community of Lavaille in rural France, uses the same argument. Reed-Danahay observes that friendship ties are neither separable from kinship relations nor are they merely a "handmaiden" to the kinship system. She explores different patterns of friendship among men and women, during adolescence and adulthood, in order to trace the formation of individual and social meanings of friendship, how they vary and persist over the course of life, and how they "help form crosscutting ties that promote concepts of local attachment that go beyond that of the family and farm" (Bell and Coleman 1999:152). To Reed-Danahay, kinship and friendship are highly overlapping, in the sense that they both contribute to the process of cultural production of attachment to locality in the face of "economic problems and the lure of the city" (Bell and Coleman 1999:7). Throughout Reed-Danahay's fieldwork there is a constant process of co-production (by kin and friends) of imaginaries of sociality and intimacy, which strikingly echoes a familiar conception of sociality in the Egyptian context. I am instantly reminded of a very well-known Egyptian proverb: *ana wa akhouya 'ala ibn 'ammi, wa ana wa ibn 'ammi 'ala al-gharib* (My brother and I against my cousin;

my cousin and I against the stranger). This proverb, while it does not include the figure of the friend, is pertinent to the previous argument. It came to mind because it expresses the typical scale of sociality in which social relationships are ordered according to the grammars of hierarchy pertaining to kin relations. These grammars are more vertical than horizontal; they describe a certain hierarchical order inherent in family structures that persist even when solidarity is called for.

The point I am suggesting here is how fluid and interactive the roles, categories, and metaphors of closeness/intimacy/sociality are, and that the positions they take vis-à-vis each other depend largely on the contextual framing and reasoning in which they are embedded and articulated. In the complex and dynamic Egyptian social environment, which is reflected in Egyptian everyday language, the overlappings and intersections of roles are endless, making it difficult to clearly demarcate friendship from family. Close friends tend to verbally grant each other the status of sister or brother, while familial relationships use idioms of friendship to describe a particular intimacy in the bond between the members; it is a way to say that they share not just blood, but also amity, harmony, acceptance, understanding, mutual trust, and a sense of bondedness that is willed, not enforced (see also Herman 1987 and Pitt-Rivers 1973). This observation is not intended as an all-encompassing theory on the interconnectedness of the two different forms of social relationships, but rather to point at how the rigid distinctions between kinship and friendship present in Western models of friendship do not hold in other contexts, in this case the contemporary Egyptian one. At the same time, this perspective proposes extending the ethnographic gaze beyond its traditional focus on Western societies, and highlighting the importance of thinking about and through friendship in non-Western contexts. It also points to the myriad ways of conceptualizing friendship apart from listing contrasts with kinship structures and family relations, since the categories need not be mutually exclusive (Bunnell et al. 2012:9).

Another important contribution from the field of anthropology is a volume entitled *The Ways of Friendship: Anthropological Perspectives* (2010) edited by Amit Desai and Evan Killick. The book is a collection of eight ethnographies conducted in various parts of the world, such as central India, rural South China, Lebanon, and South Africa, with its main focus on the diversity of meanings attached to friendship across different cultures. By focusing on local ideas, practices, and manifestations of friendship in the everyday life, most of the authors wish to investigate "the ways in which friendship acts to express fixity and fluidity in diverse social world" (Desai and Killick 2010:1). The authors devote their entire analytic attention to friendship, committing themselves to avoid the imposition of Western conceptions on "other places and people" (2010:15). They attempt to do so "by opening up the definition of friendship as widely as possible to include a variety of relationships—patron-client, childhood friends, ritual friends—in order to draw out the social importance of these types of relationships and the things that they offer" (2010:15). For example, they argue against the presumed generality attached to encompassing notions like "relatedness" (2010:5). Such encompassing concepts, as the editors argue in the introduction, tend to mask the distinctions between the different forms and purposes of relating, hence loosening up "the boundaries that people might themselves posit in the articulation of those relationships" (2010:5). Desai and Killick make it clear in the introduction that the different 'local' approaches to and articulations of friendship, the spaces, histories, and ideologies that shape the constitution of friendship as a particular social bond, lie at the heart of the anthropological analyses in this volume. However, most of the ethnographic endeavors in this book in fact stick to the significance of kinship framework, rather than work beyond it.

While it is crucial to identify and acknowledge the contingent, intersectional, and complementary entanglement of kinship/friendship relationships, balanced attention should be paid to the emotional and affective states between individuals, as well as within larger structural affinities that impact the establishment of friendships. The messiness and dynamism of the production and reproduction of social relations in any given context demands that we cultivate acute sensibilities to not only "the circumstances, conditions and barriers under which friendships are formed, encouraged, sustained and dismantled" but also to the affective registers and atmospheres that surround them (Kathiravelu 2013:7). It is extremely important to pay attention to how widely the use and understanding of the term "friend" varies with context. In some cases it is applied (granted, in a way) only to intimates who have achieved a particular status of trustworthiness, in other cases it refers to an interplay of characterizations, where schoolmates, workmates, and neighbors are sometimes called "friends." Drawing on Laavanya Kathiravelu (2013), I believe that one of the ways to grapple with these questions and arrive at a more nuanced understanding of friendship is to trace people's own characterizations of friendships, as Biehl and Locke advise us (2017). In other words, we must "listen carefully and notice swerves, follow leads and trajectories, and translate these movements into thought and writing" (Biehl and Locke 2017:xi). I am interested in following the articulations, expressions, constructions, and potentials of friendship at the moment of enactment, "beginning in the midst of social life, its rhythms, affects, surprises (from the trivial to the tragic), and urgencies" (Biehl and Locke 2017:ix). Practices and dynamics between friends in the everyday express particular grammars of intimacy that are specific to their time and place, while they can also act as effective lenses through which wider social, cultural, political, and material conditions of being and becoming can be captured.

Situating Friendship: Atmospheres, Pockets, and Infrastructures of Sociality

Reflecting on the fieldwork conducted for this study, one of the most striking facts is how temporally spread out it is; it does not have a clear starting point in time. I do know that my analytic and conceptual attention to (and eventually investment in) in friendship began to take a formal turn in 2016. Yet the stories and encounters of friendship have been ongoing throughout my entire life. The lives of the friends among and with whom I conducted interviews, walks, and trips are constantly changing, in motion, becoming otherwise, as are our selves and our friendships. The challenge lies in finding a way in which to speak of friendship that does not reduce or constrain the open-ended nature of the lifeworlds of friends themselves and of their friendships.

Geographically speaking, the birthplace of my ethnographic project is Cairo and Alexandria, two cities that have, over the past few decades, undergone a fierce series of transformations on multiple levels (political, economic, cultural, and infrastructural). As a result, the very fabric of life in these two places is composed mostly of polyphonies and stories of surprise and unpredictability, which demands a willingness and an openness in thinking and writing to trace people's trajectories as they continuously (re)figure their relationship to the world and to each other. I primarily aim for a mode of writing that resembles living; it is active, breathing, and changing, because it remains connected to the mysterious and unpredictable unfolding of the times that it witnesses and in which it is inevitably implicated. Biehl and Locke call this process an "ethnographic open system":

> *Through fieldwork, we become a part of ethnographic open systems and are folded into lives, relationships, and swerves across time and space. These systems hold us in a kind of unfinished proximity with one another, retreating and reemerging, engendering unanticipated connections and reconfigurations, never definitively closed off nor decisively transformational. Ethnographic open systems tether us to other selves and worlds and destabilize the temporal and spatial boundaries of an imagined field we leave behind.* (Biehl and Locke 2017:32)

Atmospheres. The particularities, ambiguities, and ambivalences inherent in the different lifeworlds of human beings, including their social formations, thus have to be understood in relation to their cultural, politico-economic, linguistic, historical, and geopolitical context, or the wider macrocosm in which they are grounded (Jackson 2012). I would like to expand on Jackson's argument by bringing the cultural theorist Lauren Berlant and the inspiring anthropologist Kathleen Stewart into the conversation. Both thinkers call for cultivation of an ethnographic sensibility: a sensibility of attending to the world, of writing the world in a manner that is attuned to the charged atmospheres of everyday life. In Stewart's words: "to pull academic attunements into tricky alignment with the amazing, sometimes eventful, sometimes buoyant, sometimes endured, sometimes so sad, always commonplace labor of becoming sentient to a world's work, bodies, rhythms, and ways of being in noise and light and space" (Stewart 2011:445). Like Jackson, Stewart highlights the need to develop theory out of and with stories, by attuning one's senses to the emergent labors, imaginaries, and potential ways of living in, through, and between things. Attending to the surrounding atmosphere, according to Stewart, is about being alert to the rhythms and refrains hanging in the air; it is the labor of attending to emergent forces in the course of the ordinary as they reside in the everyday life of experiences, intimacies, conditions, things, dreams, frustrations, landscapes, hopes, imaginaries, and sensory experiences (Stewart 2011).

Enmeshed in conditions of political violence, financial hardship, environmental crisis, and infrastructural breakdown, the stories we live and share are at the same time material and political as much as they are personal and ethical; "neither the personal nor the political, the particular or the abstract, senses of 'subjectivity' can be postulated as prior. They are mutually arising; each is the condition of the possibility of the other" (Jackson 2012:6). Hence, parallel to the failure of the normative life-organizing structures, we confront a collapse of ideal forms of the so-called "good life." In Berlant's words, this situation opens up a problem or a lag in apprehension, a question on how to live, a threat that is sensed materially, as well as affectively, to the sense of ongoingness in the durational present (Berlant 2008b). This pushes me to think deeper and further about the ways in which a shared alienation, estrangement, or detachment can actually become the very foundation of a social and subjective formation or imaginary. This alienation might be a rupture in life, or a certain displacement or dispossession, a loss, a breakdown, or a turning point where "life as we know it" comes to an end. Here, friendship provides a potential, a promise or a possibility of an attachment in which one will feel held, grounded in the world by relationality—though not necessarily a good relationality. Berlant's view of intimacy involves a longing for a narrative about something shared, "a story about both oneself and others that will turn out in a particular way" (Berlant 1998:281). She describes the drive toward it as wild, unpredictable, and scattered (284). This drive creates a space around it through practices, the space acting as an affective register that people can rely on and return to, and that would hold a space for them in return to produce something, though frequently that "something" will not be history in its ordinary sense, and not always "something" of positive value (285). Through this image, Berlant asks us to see with her the possibility of a political subjectivity that lives with its fragility and still manages to build a world (see also Haraway 2016).

In this shared atmosphere of fragility, friendship looms as a possibility, a collaborative project of reinventing and reproducing ways of living life while also transforming and being transformed in reciprocity. The atmospheres that enfold the makings as well as the breakings of friendships must be always be attended to and analyzed, because it is important to understand the larger social-material-affective-political register in which those relationships are formed, lived, and maintained. Friendship takes place between particular people, in specific contexts, places, and times; the encounter opens a person to another in a relation that blurs and cuts across boundaries, interweaving the self and the other, the public and the private, the personal and the collective, while achieving a mutual shaping of surfaces. Learning to lean on another is awkward and risky; learning to spin, fall, and hang onto another is also learning to be open and take leaps. The risk contains an element of unknowability that is definitely a part of the relationship, yet the leaping into this unknowability is an experience of learning: "to open up the encounter in order to learn—without an expectation of fully accessing—a stranger's thick histories and complex positionings in time and space" (Nagar 2014:5).

> *The affective subject is a person who waits in the company of others for things to arrive, one who learns to sense out what's coming and what forms it might take, one who aims to notice what crystallizes and how things ricochet and rebound in a social-natural-aesthetic ecology of compositions and thresholds of expressivity. For the affective subject, there is always the weight of the world in what can be hoped for and what must be feared, in what flourishes and what matters.* (Stewart 2017:194)

Pockets. The practices of intimacy unfold over walks and talks, cigarette breaks, lunch breaks, co-working, co-studying, in streets, offices, homes, school and university campuses, travel routes, classrooms, airports, cafeterias, elevators, parking lots, and other happenstances. Whether short-term and transient or long-term and durable, those experiences take place not in the void but in the built environments and infrastructures, where they both witness and contain each other's beginnings as well as each other's failings and fadings. Those temporal and spatial pockets in the ordinary (and the extraordinary) life of the everyday and those fragments of sociality have to be considered always closely and in relation to one another. As will be discussed in chapter 2, by drawing on the story of a personal friendship with a young woman from Alexandria, one with whom I mentally and emotionally associate the city, I argue that our friendship gave birth to "an Alexandria" as a porous space (see Stavrides 2007), mutually constituted by sets of shared encounters of trust, imagination, and interaction. To this end I draw on the concept of urban porosity as proposed by the Greek architect, activist, and author of numerous books on spatial theories and practices, Stavros Stavrides. Stavrides builds on Walter Benjamin's concept of porosity (Benjamin 1978), or the ways in which people's actions in space (particularly cities) as well as in time overflow and thus loosen the presumed fixity of both temporal boundaries (where memories, collective as well as individual, can be shared and utilized as grounds for forming new interpretations of space) and spatial boundaries (where the city that had existed and the one that does exist in the present are simultaneously present and absent as we move inside it, existing as both reality and potentiality). These practices produce what Stavrides calls "threshold spaces; in between areas that relate rather than separate" (Stavrides 2007:1). "In the unexpected connections realized by these thresholds, otherness emerges, not only as a threat but also as a promise" (Stavrides 2007:3).

Infrastructures.

> *What freedoms does this city air produce? What dream-world alongside catastrophe is there here? What power of fantasy, outside of its relentless fantasies of fear, does a city like this possess? What "profane illumination" can it still offer?* (Abourahme 2014:580)

One of the promises friendship offers is a fluidity of movement across borderlines and boundaries in everyday urban life. An embodied relation, it provides the potential to produce a different mode of sociality that produces its own social geographies between friends. Now, if the cities (understood in terms of their physical infrastructure, policies, and economies) that contain those practices and performances are constantly becoming other than they were, we need to find ways to understand this movement and cultivate a perspective that is more decentered, multiple, and shifting. It is not only important what infrastructure brings together, how it works as a site of assemblage for bodies and actions, but equally important is how we in return are inclined toward it "so that a holding takes place" (Simone 2016:157). However, "infrastructure can't really promise anything" (Simone 2016:158), it can only instigate a "temporality 'set loose' from calculation—a process of associating place, people, institutions, finance and politics that ramifies in unanticipated ways" (2016:158). The apparently fragmented and disarticulated, sometimes disenchanting and ruinous, changes that take place in cities can and do give rise to unanticipated interactions and open up new reciprocal linkages. Drawing on AbdouMaliq Simone (2004), the notion of infrastructure could be extended directly to people's activities in the city. It acquires a more encompassing definition, in which people's ability to engage, interact, and (re)work the complex combinations of objects, practices, persons, and spaces becomes a form of promising infrastructure, as they act as platforms "providing for and reproducing life in the city" (Simone 2004:408).

The future of infrastructure, in a way similar to that of friendship, is about the spaces it opens and the potentials it makes possible—the things that, in Berlant's words, might help "maintain one's sea legs" (Berlant 2011a). Thinking about the politics of infrastructure affectively and in relation to friendship makes it possible to reimagine and revitalize the political possibilities of the urban life, making them as porous and generative as the lives we live and the spaces we inhabit. I keep recalling and retelling an incident that took place near the end of my fieldwork in Alexandria with Yasmine, one of my Alexandrian friends based in Cairo. Yasmine tremendously contributed to this research, reimagining Cairo and Alexandria through our friendship, while grounding our friendship in as well as across the two cities as we traveled. For the purpose of narrating the following incident, I will try to reconstruct the setting of the encounter, which could not possibly take place without bringing her into the conversation as a part of it.

The incident took place on 3 March 2017. I wanted to go to Alexandria and Yasmine had plans to go to spend a day or two with her family there. We decided to go together and she kindly offered to let me stay at her family home; we would take the morning train the following day back to Cairo, together. We took the 10:00 PM bus on the evening of 2 March from Abdel-Moneim Riyad. Exhausted but resisting sleep, we both were more inclined to spend the few hours of travel talking. After all, as Yasmine repeatedly stated, she was genuinely interested in what might possibly come out of my research, which neither of us knew at that point, but which both of us were optimistic about. To be more precise, I would say we were optimistic about the promise it held to tell us something about friendship in its becoming, in our becoming, something about a possibility we always desire. We spent the first couple of hours talking, for a very short time with my sound-recorder on, and then I turned it off. I did not want us to 'have' to focus on a specific topic or just one kind of experience, I wanted us to be able to 'go places' in friendship and not necessarily for the sake of the "research on friendship." We arrived at 12:45 AM (now 3 March). Yasmine's mother and stepfather were waiting to pick us up, as it would have been difficult for us to find convenient transportation to downtown at such a late hour. We were by then even more tired, cold, and cranky. Yasmine's mother came out of the car to hug her and greet me, and opened the trunk for us to throw in our backpacks so that we could sit as comfortably as possible in the car. Yasmine quickly stuffed her backpack into the trunk; I kept mine with me, and we got into the car. Yasmine and her mother began a light and humorous conversation, as I stared out of the window trying to learn as much as I could about the route so that the next time I visited Alexandria by bus I would be able to find my way around. I remember exactly what happened next. We were driving over a bridge when I heard them gasp, followed by a collective "Ahhhh, go go go!"—some strange collective utterances that did not make much sense to me, but were obviously a response to something that they all knew or saw and that I missed. I looked at Yasmine to ask her what it was all about, but before she could respond, her stepfather suddenly hit the brakes as two police officers blocked the road with metal barricades. Yasmine started to explain to me, while all of them were laughing about their curious outbursts. The three of them were well aware that this street gets blocked by the police every night after midnight for security purposes. This was a relatively new pattern that started with the recent construction of the new building for the Alexandria Security Directorate. Yasmine pointed at the building and told me, "Here, look, it's new . . . this street was nothing like this before." It took me a minute to grasp the situation. Meanwhile, they all laughed that "But we were so close to passing! We were just a few seconds from it!!" Our car was now the second in what became a line of cars, all of which now had to be redirected to an alternative narrow and bumpy route. The first car had a brief chat with the police officer, who let him pass, which infuriated Yasmine's stepfather. He complained briefly about how horrid that "alternative" street is, full of bumps and sewers, anything but a smooth ride. He decided to object to the officer and see whether we could pass, too. The officer refused, telling him, "Khalas . . . 1:00 AM . . . you all know the rules." By then it was around 1:05 AM. The stepfather referred to the first car to make his case, in a polite yet persistent manner: "Let us pass, you just let him, so do the same for us and let us pass." After a brief hesitation, the officer did. The stepfather was satisfied, everyone else was in quiet anticipation. "The thrill of the adventure ended the moment the barricades outraced us!" said Yasmine.

I find this small incident incredibly telling of the ways in which informal yet official, known yet undeclared, volatile but also mandatory and enforced rules and structures are constantly revealed, sensed, and negotiated in emerging encounters of sociality. Learning about a city is also a process of unlearning, grasped always in relation to another who is unlearning and relearning as well. One can start by asking about the absences as well as the presences: What was (or was not) here before this? Why is it not here any more? One can start asking about the barricades and how to navigate their presence when they block one's way, what time they are put up and how to remember to arrive always a minute earlier. One needs to be able to notice the humor steeped in the everyday life of frustration, the vague gestures of exasperation and outrage, the gasps, the sighs, "the moments of disturbance before form provides an anchor" (Berlant 2014:3). One needs to cultivate a visual aptitude not only for the names of the streets and the bridges, but for the handwritten signs that denote neighborhoods and addresses. To borrow the phrasing of Berlant: "how the ongoingness of life produces an energetics of endurance—through touch, proximity, and conversation that's both narrative (against the state and for the collectivity's self-adherence) and eruptive in particular moments of pleasure" (Berlant 2014:3).

To Attune, to Attend, to Accompany: Learning by Being With, Within, Without

To listen and to tell a rush of stories is a method. (Tsing 2015:65)

I map Alexandria by the homes and the neighborhoods where my friends live, and by the streets we walk and the roads we take, and by the places of our gathering. I move through Cairo with my cellphone glued to my ear to be accompanied by the voices of my friends as we share the minutiae and trivia of our days. They tag along as I move through that which unfolds into happenings, big and small, some joyous, others tragic, and everything on the spectrum between. I have long thought about the ways in which looking at friendship from an anthropological lens could be achieved without violating, reducing, or defacing its extremely sensitive and complex nature. It is personal yet collective, fluid yet generative, intimate yet in many ways explicit. It is certainly a relationship that involves motion and fluidity; hence tracing it will be a matter of tracing associations and "following the actors themselves" (Latour 2005:12). In my opinion, it is the sort of ethnography that has to be experienced and written with friends, and co-constructed, slowly, by friends in nothing short of a dialogic interaction and an ongoing conversation. I believe that this dialogic mode of thinking and writing has the potential to open up new modes of attention to people's art of existence and of practices of world-making, in a manner that that does not seek to limit the contingent nature of human action and interaction. What it ultimately renders possible is a promise that the lifeworlds of our collaborators and friends, their histories and trajectories, their worldly fabrications and the knowledges they fashion, can indeed create new modes of theory and new figures of thought, radically profound and powerful.

As Paul Ricoeur expressed it in his last written work, our goal is not an identification with the other, which is, anyway, "neither possible nor desirable," but "an accompanying that means no one will have to live or die alone" (quoted in Jackson 2012:278).

Being with(in)/becoming with(out). "I think of anthropology as a process of coming home" (Ingold 2017a:127). A focus on the everyday enactments of friendship necessitates a mode of interrogation that is embodied, affective, and interactive in order to keep pace with the ebbs and flows of friendships' formations and dissolutions. As Joao Biehl and Peter Locke, drawing on Deleuze, have argued in their book *Unfinished* (2017), ethnography should always start in the midst of social life, amidst situations, objects, connections, habits, gestures, expressions, and ambivalences grounded in people's utterances as well as silences, in attachments and threats, daily rhythms, in their own characterizations of themselves, others, and the world. What the "world" here denotes is an ever-shifting assemblage of becomings: ways of living, adjusting, and carrying on in the unfolding historical present. As ethnographers of the contemporary, it is important to recognize the ways in which we are caught up in the very same webs of suspension, struggle, and precariousness as unfinished as our collaborators, as stuck and as hopeful. The challenge at hand is the urgency of reflective and interactive thought and theory that are able to begin with the contingent, the incoherent, and the awkward messiness of being-in-proximity to another without a "plan." As modern "subjects" in the neoliberal age, we have not been allowed to imagine the possibility of a world without plans, we have not been trained to care, to be tender in relation to something without the dread of displacement, dispossession, and the future-to-come. However, I argue that one of the ways in which ethnography might be able to "honor what's tender" (Berlant 2012a:5) is to work with and take in (with extreme care, empathy, and seriousness) the incoherence and indeterminacy of the immediate and the plasticity of subjects as they negotiate their complex realities in ways that are not given and hence not possibly foreseeable.

I will end this section with a long but astounding quote from Lauren Berlant, whose voice shapes so much of the atmosphere of this manuscript.

What is politics in all this? Is the idiom of care and the ambition to be tender toward one's objects and object-worlds a refusal of the massive violence of power, or a refusal to respond to power in its own idiom? To me the point of taking the risk of invention, of genuine experimentality, is not only to fail better, but to release my creativity from reproducing an absorbing repetition that goes nowhere apart from confirming that I am still who I was. . . . Thinking politics affectively makes it possible to reinvest, to multiply, to enrich the political without producing the bad feeling, the ugly feelings of being always muddied up with incommensurate aims and attachments, without which there would be no worlding. Doing it together but non-normatively releases us from the isolation of reinventing the world minute by minute, time after time. Being alive beyond the conventions means not only helping each other improvise in the middle of demands to attend, attune, be right, and be good, but also symbolizing the alternative routes we might dig, collectively, not to reproduce the ruts in which, in a heavy rain, we might drown. (Berlant 2012a:6)

The story of friendship is and always has been a personal one. I am aware of my own implication in friendship as a mode of sociality that has been and continues to be an extremely significant part of my life. Hence, in this work, others' stories will have to be interwoven with mine, others' voices fused with mine, and there is no way to escape that. The style of doing and writing ethnography I am aiming for attempts to embrace the overlapping of lifeways, the multiple layers of dialogue, emotion, embodiment, and consciousness, while also blurring the presupposed clear-cut distinctions between the self/other, home/ field, private/public. As Anna Tsing proposes on the indeterminacy and contingency of the self–other encounter, "The evolution of our 'selves' is already polluted by histories of encounter; we are mixed up with others before we even begin any new collaboration" (Tsing 2015:55).

Plan of the Work

In the chapters that follow I present different threads, theories, conditions, stories, encounters, characters, dynamics in and through various instances of friendship. In chapter 2 I attempt to demonstrate the larger mise en scene, the space-time interval in which I poke and engage different social ties, namely friendship and the family. It is important to capture, though without freezing, the context in all its complexity, for the reader to be able to trace the ubiquity of the historical present. Precarity is a state of being and also an ongoing crisis and is not a simple thing to describe, but so are people's ways of navigating it. The ties that form and those that break, and the many layers in between, are to a large extent the subject matter of chapter 2.

Chapter 3 deals with friends in/and cities, precisely the cities of Cairo and Alexandria. Co-constructed with Nadia, the chapter traces the beginning of our friendship and follows its unfolding over the years. It also digs deeper into the question of how cities can be looked at from the lens of friendship. What accounts of space and place emerge out of relations and relationalities between friends? How do cities become lived experiences through friendship walks and talks? I argue that by taking friends' experiences in and perceptions of cities seriously, something presents itself to us: an epistemological novelty. Friends constantly navigate their cities together, improvise and invent, re-member and re-create their routes and pathways. By examining these processes, I ask whether these accounts by friends can together constitute a possible archive, one of "flesh and blood."[4] What such an archive can open up for us, and how we can read the city differently through it, are some of the questions I tackle in chapter 3.

In chapter 4 I engage with philosophies on friendship by accompanying friendships on screen. I chose a few recent Egyptian artworks produced in the past 10 years and followed the portrayal of the friendships between the protagonists in them. The main aim is to examine the "representations" of friendship to the larger audience, and the connotations there are. The characters, plot, tensions, and twists of those works do provide a significant understanding of how friendship might be viewed, comprehended, and also judged. I deployed the dramatic tensions existent in the storylines of those works to emphasize and highlight the omnipresence of moments of ruptures between friends. How and when do these breakages/fractures happen? What triggers them and how do friends move from there, or rather not? Equally interesting is to pursue a nuanced reading of these works in so far as they are adamant on producing singular and definitive viewpoints on the relationship of friendship. The characters in these works also enable me to explore the difficulties of friendship in terms of the vulnerability that coexists with intimacy.

Friends constitute the final chapter. In chapter 5 I decided to devote a sufficient textual space for friends to articulate their own understandings, epiphanies, and conceptions of friendship. Some started with a

---

4   By Haytham Wardani in an email to me on thinking together about and with friendship.

song, others with an incident or a memory, and others with a joke. This chapter is a tribute to what we unmake and make again, using our own words, selves, vocabularies, narratives, memories, and philosophies. The chapter pokes the potential of friendship, while also tracing the contours of its limitations.

The ethnographic practice I am adopting involves a back-and-forth movement between introspection into the vulnerable self, and a committed reflection on its situation, carried across the surrounding socialities, objects, institutions, laws, atmospheres, and infrastructures, and both the proliferation and the death of possibilities. Through the notion, practice, and possibility of friendship I wish to explore how experiences of intimacy, companionship, and collaboration can be seen as a resource for new insights into the ways in which affects and effects of the everyday are absorbed, shared, circulated, and held or dispensed. I hear Anna Tsing's whisper to us, daring and promising, like Alice in Wonderland, leading us on what seems to be an endlessly long and dark tunnel: the blasted landscapes of life capitalism. It is not easy to know how to make a life at the end(s) of the world, but luckily, as she says, "there is still company." I join her in her prayer that perhaps it is still possible to "catch the scent of the latent commons—and the elusive autumn aroma" (Tsing 2015:391).

CHAPTER 2

While We're Here, Pass This with Me: On the Project of Friendship in a Present of Ruins

> *Sometimes common entanglements emerge not from human plans but despite them. It is not even the undoing of plans, but rather the unaccounted for in their doing that offers possibilities for elusive moments of living in common. . . . Assembling assets, we ignore the common— even when it pervades the assembly. Yet the unnoticed, too, can be a site for potential allies.* (Tsing 2015:371)

On more than one level, the historical present is a mess. Most people are striving to have a life that actually feels like a life. Juggling work and everything else happens at the cost of one's spirit. Capacities and practices of self-care and personal well-being are overshadowed by the harsh routines and disciplinary patterns needed to sustain a living in the current era of neoliberal restructuring. Moreover, under neoliberalism, notions of self-care are more often than not seen as an individual responsibility devoid of any connection with building communities. In his book *Friendship in an Age of Economics: Resisting the Forces of Neoliberalism* (2012), Todd May provides an in-depth analysis of the unfolding themes and phenomena that underlie the "neoliberal" moment in which we live. May begins by drawing our attention to the fact that our social worlds are by no means immune to or divorced from the context in which we find each other and ourselves. While we should not take "neoliberalism" to be the all-encompassing rubric under which the ongoing historical present might be merely observed and studied, it becomes important to identify how the term "neoliberalism," as a moment in

time, an atmosphere, a collective affect, a set of conditions and consequences, shapes much of who we are, with ourselves and with one
another, "and of the difficulty and perhaps even the darkness of who we
are asked to be" (May 2012:4).

"What I am calling neoliberalism is an emerging and intersecting
set of practices, embedded in a particular economic orientation, that
has contributed much into making us who we are today" (May 2012:4).
One of the ways in which May defines neoliberalism is as the current
complete reliance of the governments on the mechanisms of the capitalist market, promoting the view that it is the best and most efficient
system for an economy to be run. In this process, one that has been
happening over the past 30 or 40 years, the social relationships between
people have inevitably been contaminated and considerably altered. It
is not that what we live and experience is utterly and completely pre-
defined by the larger economic context hovering over us, but rather how
neoliberalism as a project has given birth to a set of social, spatial, economic, cultural, and political conditions that largely mold our ways of
living. Taking this discussion further, May traces how the current set of
neoliberal forces and conditions impinge upon individuals, giving rise to
the particular figures characteristic of our time, particularly those of the
"consumer" and the "entrepreneur." May particularly stresses that those
two figures are not and should not be thought of as the sole or exhaus-
tive figural legacy of neoliberalism, yet through them, one might be able
to gain a better understanding of the larger project of normalization
that is intimately tied to the aims of state capitalism. The figure of the
consumer is not an expression of merely someone who consumes, but
rather someone whose identity is deeply tied to their activity as a consumer—that is, consumption largely determines who they "are," it does
not stop at what they "do." As for the figure of the entrepreneur, May
points at a character that essentially lives by a constant and frivolous
engagement with the activity of investment toward the future, continuously seeking the best return or payoff for a given investment of material
or time (May 2012:44). May uses these figures in order to determine
how and how much our current patterns of living, being, and interacting can tell us about the magnitude and the intensity of the effect of
neoliberalism on our lives. While the figures do in fact represent acute
manifestations or outcomes of the intersection between neoliberalism

and our humanity, they lack the confusion, the puzzlement, the uncertainty, and the chaotic murkiness of contemporary existence.

My State of Being Is Walking: *Mashy al-hal/Mashya*

More often than not, when asked about our "day," we struggle for words and end up stuttering. We express ourselves in a splintered and confused language that reflects how worn out we feel and how fragmented our days are. The ability to control our own lives in terms of "time" is becoming an impossible dream, because for most of us, economic survival depends on "work," on "submission to the daily grind" (Frayne 2015:18), with all the moral, material, and political pressures that bear down on the worker throughout the "working day." Speaking from where I am in the world, in Cairo the everyday is a brutal and somewhat fierce encounter, one that is ever changing, and that carries within it possibilities: sometimes threats, and at other times promises of excess that sometimes translate into moments or incidents of a transformative hope, or hope for transformation. At other times, these same promises weigh on the present as a never-ending despair, a perpetual sense of exhaustion. In the stuttering language of everyday, the question of how one is doing, "*Ezzay-yek/ak?*" in 'Ammiya (colloquial Egyptian Arabic), is usually answered by "*Mashya*" or "*Mashy al-hal,*" "My state of being is walking." As Ghassan Hage states, the language of articulation of one's own well-being is in most cases tied to a notion of movement, either metaphorical or physical. As opposed to "stuckedness" (Hage 2009), walking represents a language of movement, of well-being, that is more than a mere linguistic figure of speech, but conveys a sense that "when a person feels well they actually imagine and feel that they are moving well" (98).

The thick and ongoing historical present, with its deteriorating social, political, economic, and environmental conditions, is most eloquently described by Lauren Berlant as a mediated affect of "crisis ordinariness." In *Cruel Optimism* (2011a), Berlant inspired me to read the patterns and rhythms of adjustment that people constantly experience in moments of transition and transaction, the ways in which bodies, individually and collectively, sense and respond to glitches in the reproduction of life in the historical present. The glitch, in Berlant's words, is "an interruption within transition, a troubled transmission" (2016:393). She writes,

I want to show how transactions of the body of the aestheticized or mediated subject absorb, register, reenact, refigure, and make possible a political understanding of shifts and hiccups in the relations among structural forces that alter a class' sense of things, its sensing of things. It involves encountering what it feels like to be in the middle of a shift and to use reconfigurations of manner amid the persistence of the body in the world to embody not the continuities of institutionalized history but something incoherent or uncongealed in the ongoing activity of the social. It is to see what is happening to systems of self-intelligibility through watching subjects getting, losing, and keeping their bearing within a thick present. (Berlant 2011a:198)

The "hiccups" are interruptions or suspensions of norms of the reproduction of life that occur on several registers. Precarity here reveals an impasse that circulates through diverse locales and bodies (Berlant 2011a:199). One experiences, works out, and adapts to the historical present as a "holding station that doesn't hold security but opens out into anxiety, that dogpaddling around a space whose contours remain obscure" —in Berlant's terms, an "impasse" (Berlant 2011a:200). The impasse is the present. It is a stretch of time, a temporal structure, a moment of radical contingency, when the conventional imaginaries and fantasies of the good life start to fray and the traditional infrastructures for reproducing life as we know it begin to dissolve.

My ethnography takes place in two cities that have been in flux for decades, undergoing extreme change. In both Cairo and Alexandria, it is not hard to notice the intensified levels of anxiety and uneasiness, of both the state and the people, stemming from and pouring into a vast range of conditions of precarity and insecurity. One thing that particularly added to this atmosphere of vulnerability, even fear, was the economic turbulence that followed the Egyptian government's devaluation of the Egyptian pound in November 2016. This collective detachment of us, as subjects, from our familiar spending habits can easily be felt in the streets and inside the comfort of homes, where "the urgencies of livelihood are worked out all over again, without assurances of futurity, but nevertheless proceeding via durable norms of adaptation" (Berlant 2011a:200). Almost everyone is faced with repeated price increases of every single commodity while incomes remain the same, and thus has less and less value. Meanwhile, moving through the cities, one is constantly stunned by the continual infrastructural transformations executed by the state. The pace is very quick, and the implementation abrupt, difficult to apprehend. And all of it is happening in a gloom of intense political uncertainty and distress, living under a military dictatorship.

Some of the most striking moments of my ethnographic interviews with Alexandrian friends were those that revealed their frustrating, alienating, and distressing experience of the infrastructural changes happening in their home city. The newly built bridge in the Sidi Gaber area of Alexandria, built by the Egyptian military in 2017, is one sudden and even bizarre example.

"It's so weird; I hate it."
"It doesn't feel normal to see the sea from above; it's pointless and ugly. It frustrates me very much every single time I have to pass it or drive over it."
"I can't believe it, the entire neighborhood is nothing like what it used to be. Unbelievable!"
"I feel this is a different city from the one I have always known."

These are few spontaneous opinions about the bridge in Sidi Gaber expressed by my Alexandrian friends. The third comment is from a friend whom I was with when he encountered the bridge for the first time in July 2017, when it was under construction. He was from Alexandria but lived in Cairo, had not been in Alexandria for months, and thus had heard about but never seen the bridge-in-the-making. He was in a state of shock, incomprehension, peculiar denial, and downheartedness. The precarity and vagueness of the scene as it lives in me do not arise only from the intensity of the encounter itself, that summer afternoon when we walked from the Alexandria train station to a café in Sidi Gaber to have breakfast and hang out with friends. The agony that he experienced during our walk, his wandering eyes and his unsettled body, are also preserved by a third friend. We both saw his troubled and confounded looks, and we walked next to him, in an attempt perhaps to mend his sense of brokenness and alienation by walking through it together. We did not have the same feelings as he about the Sidi Gaber neighborhood; we have never lived there, not even close to it, and our historical relatedness to it is weak because we are both Cairenes, but we could certainly understand, or imagine we understood. We were moved by something that did not belong to us, yet to some extent we know how it feels. However, I cannot say that our "walk of friends" was of any consolation to our Alexandrian friend. I do not think that any relationship has the capability of grounding a person on a land of shifting sands. Let me also add that the shifting-ness was not limited to the surrounding environment. This person and I are no longer a part of each others' lives, and this person and our third friend are no longer part of each others' lives, for a variety of reasons that are a mesh of personal and impersonal disappointments and failures. Perhaps we knew back then something about the unshareability and the ungraspability of pain, as Sara Ahmed suggests in *The Cultural Politics of Emotion* (2014:31). Our joint experience was not so much based on the possibility that we could ease or heal his pain, but rather that we could live and walk together, bearing witness to the pain, confusion, and sadness that enfolded our relationship at that moment.

> *In fact, we must love the visions we have, if there is any point to having them. We must be invested in them, whilst open to ways in which they fail to be translated into objects that can secure our ground in the world. We need to be invested in the images of a different kind of world and act upon those investments in how we love our loves, and how we live our lives, at the same time as we give ourselves up and over to the possibility that we might get it wrong, or that the world that we are in might change its shape.* (Ahmed 2014:141)

If everyone feels perplexed, or at the very least shaky, in an environment of unfathomable or undesirable changes, what does it mean to lean on one's friends? In this chapter I will focus on the role of intimacy, and in particular on friendship, as a mode of relating and responding to others with whom we share a particular vulnerable present. As a social bond, friendship has existed everywhere and at all times, grounded, configured, and practiced differently according to the historical, cultural, economic, social, and political context within which it is embedded. Generative and flawed, active and irregular as it is, I would like to trace the project of friendship, in an attempt to glimpse, even if momentarily and fleetingly, what it can hold and what it can offer. The scene is one of "muddling through with others" (Tsing 2015:385), and it is filled with flows, intensities, encounters, surprises, and flashes of hope, as well as exhaustion, weariness, and anxiety. How can we look at, think through, and write about survival as a collaborative project in which friends do not "bridge over" but rather "pass this," among and alongside each other?

I Don't Feel at Home in This World Any More, or, How Predictable Is Precarity?

"Precarity means not being able to plan," writes Anna Tsing (2015) in her beautiful book *The Mushroom at the End of the World*, in which she elegantly pours out stories of divergence as well as collaboration among humans, non-human subjects, and landscapes in a world that is falling apart under contemporary capitalism. Tsing chooses to take the knot that is the mess of the world, the mesh of entanglements, as it is, and examine the potentialities laid out behind the interwoven strands. The reader travels on a journey with Tsing, reflecting upon the creative and awkward entanglements, interactions, connections, and collaborations of the social on both local and global levels at a time when things are "messy" and "difficult." When living with the unforeseeable, with contingency, is no longer an exception or an abnormal, temporally bounded affect, the present becomes a lived problematic that is "charged with intensity" (Stewart 2017:194). In these conditions, the way that things unfold and play out is almost always a surprise. In fact, precarity has stretched out and swallowed us all. To live in the belly of the whale called precarity is no longer an unlikely and far-fetched nightmare, but rather a lifeworld, or a composition of circumstances, stirrings, possibilities, threats, assemblages, orderings and reorderings, openings and foreclosures, circuits of force and form in an ongoing state of transition.

In the belly of the whale of precarity, it is dark, ambiguous, and mostly frightening, yet one is not alone. You wait humbly in the ambiguity for "some uncharitable new current of life to stir" (Eagleton 2015:67). After some time in the dark you usually lose your balance, you start to tremble, you get dizzy and lose your equilibrium, you stumble and almost fall, and sometimes, or even most of the time, you regain your balance by using some help. A support body, a support system. You hold hands with the person next to you, you lean on them, you whisper or scream, you ask for help. This movement, this plea for help, can be read as an openness to the transformative potentiality of the encounter with the other, the stranger next to you who might become a friend and might not. In all cases, with the intensified affect of fear or uncertainty comes "a heightened sense of belonging with other people" (2015:6). You remind yourself that you are not alone in this, and that reminder alone brings a sense of potential to the situation.

Drawing once again on Lauren Berlant, the collectively held sense of glitch requires not only training in contingency management, but finding of one's footing in new manners of being (2011a:196). A footing is a grounding in the world, a carving of a place in the world, an inhabitance, and a wager against the world that it might, after all, be, worth it. It can be said that intimacy, particularly between friends, acts as a possibility, a potential space that "links the instability of individual lives to the trajectories of the collective" (Berlant 1998:283). It provides a landscape fertile enough for footings, be they affective or instrumental, embodying an "aspiration for a narrative about something shared" (Berlant 1998:281). While the fantasies associated with intimacy sometimes end up occupying the space of convention, the desire for it is not necessarily a mode of organizing life, or persons, in a particular way toward a particular goal. Rather it is a drive that produces itself relationally, gradually, through experimenting and practicing with reciprocity, responsiveness, and closeness. Friendship presents a porous sociality, "an affective space where people ought to be legitimated because they have feelings and because there is an intelligence in what they feel that *knows* something about the world that, if it were listened to, could make things better" (Berlant 2008a:13). The intimacy shared between friends provides a mode that is different from (and alternative to) that which takes place within the purview of institutions of the state and the traditional and somewhat fixed ideals of the nation, community, and citizens, as it does not necessarily stick to a canon, a utopian fantasy, or a designated end goal. Within friendship, the friend's experience of the present moment is a story that is recognized (though not necessarily identified with or related to) in a way that allows a potential sense of belonging in and by a social world. In this way, the desire for intimacy that underlies, for example, the act of complaining to one's friends about the stresses and anxieties of the everyday, or the urge to share a vague sense of discomfort and detachment, is also about a sense of potential belonging. Drawing on Berlant's argument in *The Female Complaint* (2008a), the need for intimate spheres is, in the end, a desire for a place of simplicity, a site of potential rest from the hard cold world. It is, in Berlant's words, "the constantly emplotted desire of a complex person to rework the details of her history to become a vague or simpler version of herself" because there is nothing simple about the lives lived under all of the existing vectors of subordination. It is at the end an aspiration to be "affectively recognized and emotionally important" (Berlant 2008a:7).

You Can Count on Me: Economies and Labors of Intimacy

What does it mean to be together-in-vulnerability? And is being and becoming-together not in and of itself a vulnerable position or process? As social beings, we are precisely dependent on what is "outside ourselves." Hence having a "life" is unimaginable outside the interdependence of persons and the reproduction and sustainability of social relations with other beings, both human and non-human (Butler 2009). "No man is an island" and no one comes from without. One is born to this world from within the womb of another. To be more accurate, one is essentially *brought* to this world and hence one's life is necessarily in the hands of the other from the start.

Given that the social relations that attach people to each other and to their environment are part of the conditions of possibility for life itself, it is important to add that those relations are not necessarily of love or of care, as Judith Butler argues, "but constitute obligations toward others, most of whom we cannot name and do not know, and who may or may not bear traits of familiarity to an established sense of who 'we' are" (2009:14). Living, thus, involves a certain exposure, a "laying out" to that which surrounds us. It is a precarious life that you live inside that whale's belly, but it is, at the same time, a social life. Being is being among others, and so precariousness, or the weight of the present, is experienced both within and outside this sociality. It is constantly a reciprocal and corresponding experience, in which one person relies on and also responds to the other. Those affective systems of intimacy and attachment and their "knotty entailments" are the sites where things happen. They do not change the world, they might not carry each other up and out of the whale's belly, yet they do offer flashes of another possible way of being. Intimacy provides a promise of living, of enduring life "without being torn and worn out by the labor of disappointment and the disappointment of labor" (Berlant 2010:112). This promise, I believe, takes the shape of an open bet on trust, and time, and trust over time. Trust, here, inspired by Todd May's propositions, is not the same as trading precarity for predictability. "It is not a calculation that the friend will act in certain ways," writes May. "It is instead a placing oneself in the hands of the friend. It is to let loose (without entirely abandoning) the grip of one's own cognitive orientation toward the world in favor of another's" (2012:114). Trusting a friend remains a potential, a tiny enigmatic miracle, that does not always guarantee a safe landing. Hence, the kind of trust I am describing is a bet that is constituted by and at the same time constitutive of the present moment, although we cannot say that it remains free of the weight of future expectations. Yet seen as a muddling-through-together, it is based on an attempt to imagine, and possibly to sustain, an alternative to the eerie, wrecked, wretched, and difficult experience of being in the whale's belly, in the dark.

Modes of Sociality/Intimacy: How Deep Is Your Love?

> We do not relate to the light, the earth, the air, and the warmth only with our individual sensibility and sensuality. We communicate to one another the light our eyes know, the ground that sustains our postures, and the air and the warmth with which we speak. . . . We appeal to the others to help us be at home in the alien elements into which we stray: in the drifting and nameless light and warmth of infancy, in the nocturnal depths of the erotic, and in the domain of dying where rational discourse has no longer anything to say. (Lingis 1994:184–185)

The modes and modalities of intimacy in the zone of the contemporary neoliberal world are various and diverse. There are structures of affinity that are already existent independent of our will, by which I mean the family. The family is the first and foremost form through which we learn what it means to live with and be surrounded by others. It is a fundamental placeholder that plants in most of us the basic principles of "care" and of "belonging." Many of the early attempts of classic social scientists have revolved precisely around the dynamics and positionalities of the different members of the family, as a quintessential bond that ties people together. In my own view, and throughout my own personal experience, I have over and over been troubled by what is constantly being left unsaid about familial intimacy, and more fundamentally, what goes missing in the naturalization of the family as a social unit. In other words, there are numerous limitations and considerations that are integral to as well as constitutive of one's position in and response-ability to the family as a structure and a relationship, most of which have been under-theorized or altogether left out. There is a lot of taken-for-grantedness and not much scrutiny about the standards and magnitudes of closeness, of relatedness, and of identification among family members. The mother, the father, the daughter, the son, the sister, and the brother are structural roles that are configured and reconfigured differently in different contexts, places, and times, yet there is a powerful rigidity to the expectations and outcomes that often makes them impervious to transformation.[5]

The family as a unit, as a standard for "familiarity" within the boundaries and the comfort of "home," is a largely unpacked and unquestioned social category. Much like citizenship, you are condemned to the family that you are born into, one whose purpose in the eyes of the state is to produce prosperous, good, well-behaved and well-educated members of the society, the nation, the state. The family in Egypt is mainly portrayed as a producer of generations, a guarantee of efficiency, stability, consistency, endurance, and permanence. Ultimately, the family is a part of the state apparatus, as a central site for reaffirming and transmitting stable affiliations of religion, nationality, and ethnicity by means of legal binding ties among the family members.

I do not wish to produce dogmas about the family as an inflexible and unbending authoritarian all-encompassing institution, or to imply that it is a structure that lacks all potential for creativity and inventiveness. In fact it has, at many times and for many people, demonstrated a profound ability to shatter many of the normative discourses and understandings of its codes, orders, and function(ality). Rather, I am interested in tracing the contours of what the family can and does offer, not only in terms of love, care, and support, but also in how much growth and movement

---

5   See also Michelle Obeid's work (2010) on kin relations, friendships, and sociality in the *day'a* of Arsal in Lebanon.

it is able to allow. A further question is how much affective labor is involved in the relationship, and how it is possible to de-naturalize, de-familiarize, and question the work involved in processes of "production of the soul" (Musil as cited in Hardt 1999:97). It is important to consider the caring labor that takes place in the comfort of "home" and within the familial realm, and the kinds of affects that are circulated and mobilized, producing different subjectivities and commonalities among subjects. "This commonality is not a name but a power" as both Hardt and Negri argue (Negri 1999:85), a power not of constriction or coercion but of desire. The flows and investments of desire are affective forces that drive productivity, constructing and transforming value according to the usual rhythm of a given society. Affective labor (and its productive effects) thus can be read as an expansive power that lies at the heart of our social as well as our productive life, and needs to be made more visible and legible in order for us to be able to deconstruct the taken-for-granted categories and institutions of intimacy (i.e., the family) and reassemble them in a different light, unpacking and perhaps provoking in the process fresh imaginaries of new (yet-to-come) social formations and organizations.

As Lauren Berlant argues in her book *Desire/Love* (2012b), the institutional forms of intimacy, such as the family and the married couple, have been central to shaping the modern states' narratives about the stability, security, and consistency of intimacy, more precisely the joy of intimacy. In modern states the fantasy of romantic love is deployed normatively "as a rule that legislates the boundary between a legitimate and valuable mode of living/loving and all the others" (Berlant 2012b:87). That is, those traditional forms have become conventions that act as the sole proper sites for "providing the life plot in which a subject has 'a life' and a future" (Berlant 2012b:86). This fantasy, the popular romance of "finding the one, getting married, and making a family," imposes on the public imagination, as well as in practice, a reduction of life's valid possibilities and potentials to a single route. The valorization of this "normal" desire, to love, to be loved, to belong to and fit within a romantic relationship, typically neutralizes, at least symbolically, the violence at play in the hierarchy of social and socially gendered relationships. This flattening of social power dynamics and inequalities, as Berlant points out, "suggests that structures and institutions of power can always be overcome by personal feelings, personal choices" (Berlant 2012b:108). The romantic couple is an aspiration for the utopian promise of a love that does not destabilize or threaten the very things (like identity and life) that it seeks to ameliorate. The idea of romantic love serves initially as a placeholder for the desire for happiness, companionship, and reciprocity, as a longing for an intimacy that is something other than (or above) the violence of disciplinary and institutional zones of belonging. However, it is important to think of how the normative cultural, social, and political discourses on romantic love have managed to affect the relations between "the hegemonic processes of collective life and what people typically imagine as love" (Berlant 2012b:109). The fantasy, or the fetish, of heteronormative romance affects individuals the same way the promise of national capitalism does: the stimulation of desire is driven by ideologies of choice, consent, and fulfillment. Now a love story is a story naturally believed to express the true nature, unique feelings, and happy destiny of the actors involved. However, as long as the normative narrative and institutionalized forms of sexual life organize identity for people, these love stories mainly get lived as a relation of "cruel optimism." In other words, the story becomes implicated in an optimistic attachment to "the scene of fantasy," looping in the belief that at this time, nearness to this thing will give me what I need, or will reproduce my world in just the right way (Berlant 2011b:2).

The correlation between happiness and marriage (as an indication of the good life) has been beautifully investigated by Sara Ahmed in her book *The Promise of Happiness* (2010). Ahmed argues that certain framings of nearness or belonging to an object, in this case a social bond such as marriage, family, and heterosexual intimacy, are generally preconceived as "happy objects" that contain within them the promise of future happiness. These objects, Ahmed suggests, are mobilized as such even in "the absence of happiness by filling a certain gap; we anticipate that the object will cause happiness, such that it becomes a prop that sustains the fantasy that happiness is what would follow if only we could have 'it'" (2010:32). The consonance of marriage with happiness is construed from the standing that marriage enjoys as a cause of happiness, a social ideal, or a "stopping point rather like the word *because*. . . . When *because* becomes an answer to a question the conversation can stop. . . . Happiness provides us with a full stop, a way of stopping an answer from being a question" (Ahmed 2010:203). Hence there needs to be a serious awareness of the moment when happiness turns from being the thing we want, to being the measure of the good. As Ahmed cleverly puts it, "We may need to defend our arguments by not making happiness our ground, while exposing the shakiness of happiness as a ground" (2010:204).

A friend comes onto the scene as a cluster of promises. My understanding of friendship can only be articulated in terms of the endless potentialities of surprise, accident, indeterminacy, scenes of emergence, and open-ended encounters—in Anna Tsing's words, "the very stuff of collaborative survival" (2015:43); in my own words, the here and the now of things, of the flux that is life and the act of being and living together. Whether they are long-term childhood friendships or short-term, casual, and transient ones, I argue that the project of friendship offers a space for new mutual becomings and reciprocal reproduction of selves, a space that can and does act in big and small ways against the capitalist processes of exploitation and precarization. As an "open threshold of potential" (Massumi 2015:3), a placeholder for something yet to come, the friend is a realization of "the possibility of alliance" (Federici 2008) and hence the emergence of the possibility of moving radically together—in Federici's words, "in collective confrontation" against the established orders of capitalist control and governmentality. This perpetual engagement with the other is precisely the experiment of being in the world as it unfolds, of "waiting in the company of others for things to arrive," as Kathleen Stewart so beautifully phrases it (2017:194). "There is always the weight of the world in what can be hoped for and what must be feared, in what flourishes and what matters . . . a rhythmic alteration that shimmers and dims" (195).

Friends as Polyphonic Assemblages: From Scattered Individual Melodies to Rhythmic Collective Harmonies

My Friends.
My friends without shields walk on the target It is late the windows are breaking
My friends without shoes leave What they love. Grief moves among them as a fire among Its bells My friends without clocks turn On the dial they turn. They part

My friends with names like gloves set out. Bare handed as they have lived. And nobody knows them. It is they that lay the wreaths at the milestones it is their Cups that are found at the wells. And are then chained up

My friends without feet sit by the wall Nodding to the lame orchestra Brotherhood it says on the decorations My friend without eyes sits in the rain smiling With a nest of salt in his hand

My friends without fathers or houses hear Doors opening in the darkness Whose halls announce

Behold the smoke has come home

My friends and I have in common. The present a wax bell in a wax belfry. This message telling of. Metals this. Hunger for the sake of hunger this owl in the heart And these hands one. For asking one for applause

My friends with nothing leave it behind In a box My friends without keys go out from the jails it is night They take the same road they miss. Each other they invent the same banner in the dark They ask their way only of sentries too proud to breathe

At dawn the stars on their flag will vanish

The water will turn up their footprints and the day will rise Like a monument to my. Friends the forgotten (Merwin 1969)

In living through an atmosphere of change and alterations, tyranny and corruption, injustice and oppression, where and how you spend your days depends on circumstances beyond your control. Uncertainty enfolds your life, and the goal is not to escape it, but rather to navigate your movement within it. "Unable to rely on a stable structure of community, we are thrown into shifting assemblages, which remake us as well as our others. We can't rely on the status quo; everything is in flux, including our ability to survive" (Tsing 2015:44). Being attuned to the coming-together of movements and to the emerging fields of belonging grants us a "power to" rather than a "power over" our historical present. The company of the friend and the muddling-through-together becomes a creative conversion of the divisions and breakages that capitalism repeatedly and variously engenders between people in different ways. Friendship can thus be theorized as a political movement that "meets affective modulation with affective modulation" (Massumi 2015:35), one that is primarily concerned with the re-creation of its members by producing forms of "life," "solidarity," and "belonging" outside systems of exploitation and hierarchy. Friendship as a world-making project opens possibilities for forms of recomposition and reorganization that might be better able to grapple with the forces that shape the present moment.

Friendship can be defined as a breathing, moving relation between two or more people. It does have its own set of shortcomings, flaws, and limitations, yet I believe that its imperfect nature and somewhat contingent character make it a more generous container for the messy state of things. The sustainability of a friendship depends on getting lost in different paths of growth and movement, then finding each other again in a shared and willed space of togetherness. And this is precisely why friendship matters, because it has an ability to endure the weight of the present and a chance that, sometimes, we might be embraced as we are.

CHAPTER 3

Those Who Love Me Can Take the Train: On the Becoming of Friends and the Making of Cities

Heartbeat of a Friend's Shadow (Tapeshe Sayehyeh Doust)
by Sohrab Sepeheri (2013)

The village lay some distance away, darkly outlined
Our eyes, full of local legends, evoked the moon.
Night was very close.

We were passing through streaks of mud, now dry on the road,
Ears overflowing with the chatter of open green fields,
Backs loaded with the reverberations of distant cities,
The harsh reality of the land flowing underfoot.

In our ruminations the taste of tranquility swayed from side to side.
Our shoes, which had prophetic qualities,
With a breeze ripped us off the earth.
On its own shoulder, our walking stick carried eternal spring.
At every turn of thought we each had the whole expanse of the sky.
Each movement of our hands sang with the beating of
Dawn-enraptured wings.
Our pockets full of the chirping of childhood mornings.
We were a band of enamored pilgrims, and our road
Passing by villages familiar with detachment,
Went on toward boundless clarity.

Over a pool, heads bent down of their own accord:
On our faces, night was evaporating,
The voice of the friend reached the ear of the friend.

Vignette: Those Who Love Me Can Take the Train, and Other Ordinary Affects

I was walking down the streets of downtown when I got a message on Facebook from one of the people closest to my heart. A dear friend. It was a very sweet message on an insane day. I was, as usual, caught up in the madness of *wust al-balad* (downtown). Rushing, with my large scarf carefully wrapped around my chest like a life jacket, holding my heavy bag so tightly, where I seem to carry all my belongings as if I might forget them if they do not accompany me everywhere I go. I checked the phone in a hurry and the message slowed me down for a minute. My heartbeats were very fast and loud; I could actually hear them. I couldn't help but smile, genuinely.

Guess what? I'm getting married . . . and guess where? In your favor-
ite city . . . Alexandria! Please come. It will make me very happy.

I read the message a couple of times, put the phone back in my purse, and resumed my fast-paced walking. The smile preserved itself on my face for a while. I detached from the environment for a while, and automatically drifted inside my head to craft a response that could even partially express my delight with and excitement for my friend, who was getting married to someone whom I knew he loved immensely. I decided not to text back immediately, as words were running all around inside my head. I'll wait for a better moment, I told myself.

On the morning of the wedding, 1 April 2016, six of us got together at the Ramsis train station, four young men and two young women. We took the 9:00 Cairo–Alexandria train, ready with our gowns and suits for the occasion. The ride was three hours of sharing stories. Stories about ourselves, our days, the films we watched, the friends we met, the friends we lost.

There's the promise of losing oneself in the flow of things, says Kathleen Stewart.[6]

---

6   The fragments and sentences are by Kathleen Stewart from her book *Ordinary Affects* (2007).

We couldn't escape politics. We all have friends who have been detained or imprisoned. We couldn't escape ourselves.

The train stopped in Tanta after an hour or so, and there was a moment of silence. We watched the people getting off the train, families, women, men, kids. I looked out of the window, watching my fellow passengers, now drifting strangers as they left. Right next to me was a long pole with a picture glued on the side facing me. It was a black and white poster with a picture of a young boy. On the white frame there was a telephone number, handwritten. I looked closer. I couldn't read the words. The handwriting was rather small but I could clearly see the phone number. One after the other, my friends saw the same scene, and nothing was said about it. I kept staring at the boy in the picture. He wasn't smiling. Neither was I. I looked at the friend sitting across me and asked him if he knew what this was about. He and the other friend who was sitting next to me said the same word at the same moment: "Absentee." I said, "Lost?"

We all looked at the kid in silence. Questions floated around in my head, grey clouds. I couldn't stop staring. Where might he be? Alive? Well? Afraid? Why didn't my friends say that he was "lost"; why "absentee"? Because changing one's place, or straying away from what one comes to know as home, isn't really the same thing as being lost? Because they were all trying to figure out what that picture was about just as much as I was? Home is a splintered word, I said to myself. And I tried to remember where I had read that. And instead of googling the quote, I googled "absentee": A person who is expected or required to be present at a place or event but is not.

Something huge and impersonal runs through things, but it's also mysteriously intimate and close at hand. At once abstract and concrete, it's both a distant, untouchable order of things and a claustrophobically close presence, like the experience of getting stuck in a customer service information loop every time you try to get to the bottom of things.

"'Those Who Love Me Can Take the Train.' We should use that movie title for the photo album that we'll make out of this trip, no?" The train started to move. I'm losing the kid. I was starting to get a bit delirious, but my friend's voice caught my attention. I smiled, and I whispered a loving goodbye to the kid. I hope you find the home where you belong.

And we try to forget, as if nothing happened. Just move on.

"What? What did you just say?" I asked my friend. He said "'Those Who Love Me Can Take the Train'; it's this 90s French film that I watched a few months ago, so I'm saying it would make a good title for the trip photo album since we're all traveling for that wedding . . . but no, wait, it was about friends gathered for a funeral, so no, really. We shouldn't, it's a bad omen." I liked the title very much. I asked him what the film was about. I was intrigued. He told me it's about a train ride where friends of a deceased painter gather on the way to attend his funeral, because of a request he left for them before he died. He wants to be buried in a city outside Paris, and wants those who loved him to come and bid him farewell together, by train. They don't know each other and have never met each other before, and so they are bound by nothing but their shared love for him and their shared sorrow over his loss.

We arrived at Alexandria. We had a big breakfast, split up to different apartments and hotel rooms, got into our soirée outfits, and met again. We celebrated our friend, hugged him, danced with him, took pictures of him and the bride, left and spent the rest of the evening together, then took the morning train the next day back to Cairo.

A week passed. I met the same friends one night and we went to see a film together in a downtown screening. A famous 1975 German film by Wim Wenders titled *The Wrong Move*. I think it's about loneliness, or desperation, or detachment, or the need to find oneself. "And don't lose that unrest and discontent of yours. You'll need it for writing." The film begins with this line, a mother speaking to her son. I close my eyes and I smile.

This vignette was written in 2016. In the months that followed, I decided to make more frequent visits to the city where many of my friends live, or at least come from, in an attempt to explore and look at the "cities' affect" engendered in and expressed by our friendship as itself a place, carved in time and dispersed across the cities of Cairo and Alexandria. This chapter seeks to narrate different experiences of movement and of stillness, and instances of what I call the affective dwelling. "Dwelling" here is defined by an enablement of moments of rest and stillness among conditions of change, instability, and uncertainty. In other words, how does friendship feed into and contribute to shaping our perception of place and "being-at-home" in particular places at particular times? How does friendship constitute a part of what might be defined as "the city affect"? What is dwelling, if we try to move beyond the rigid spatial aspect of the concept of dwelling? I draw on various moments of social intimacy and encounters of friendship in the cities of Cairo and Alexandria in an attempt to trace the contours of affective attachments that link friends to each other and to shifting spaces.

I chose Cairo and Alexandria because I have so many friends who are Alexandrians living in Cairo or moving between the two cities. This movement between Alexandria and Cairo carries a myriad of hopes: independence from a rigid family structure, job opportunities, wider social and professional networks. I found it important to pay attention to how the relations between the cities present themselves in conversations between friends. In this connection I will discuss three practices of friendship, on both conceptual and actual levels, that display rhythms of movement and rest. These are witnessing, staying in touch, and catching up. These practices amount to a collaborative quest for a moment of stillness, a dwelling place, that can perhaps be realized by bringing together the past, the present, and the imagined-things-to-come in an encounter of intimacy and trust.

In this analysis, "movement" is a notion that disrupts, challenges, and perhaps transcends the seemingly fixed distinctions between the "temporality" and the "spatiality" of experience. By focusing on the figure of the friend, I would like to unpack the ways in which notions of movement and rest are articulated and made sense of in ways that are spatial, temporal, and social simultaneously.

Friends constantly move together back and forth in time, revisiting their individual memories and shared histories while also projecting both personal and mutual visions and ambitions on unknown and unknowable futures. In terms of the cities themselves, living in Cairo, Alexandria, or between the two means living on shifting sands. Each of them has recently been undergoing a process of massive, often overwhelming infrastructural change implemented by the state. During

such times of transition, it is important to pay attention to the modes
of attachment, detachment, response, response-ability, and doing and
undoing of intimacies that unfold within the intensified atmosphere
of instability. "Instability" here is not meant to convey a mere sense of
insecurity about the future, but stretches to communicate a collectively
held sense that life is daily changing to something other than it was.
Hence notions of movement, dislocation, and relocation are not only
about changing one's home or making new beginnings in the lifelong
project of pursuing one's dreams, but also about the disappearances or
even the deaths of certain attachments to places in particular ways, and
the emergence of others that redefine conceptions of "being-at-home"
in the world.

This chapter will explore the themes that emerged from conversations with friends during movement between the cities of Cairo and
Alexandria, about space, time, and both of them combined in becoming.
Certainly, our conversations are shaped by our own experiences, they
are not ultimately intended to culminate in a comprehensive analysis of
how social relationships are affected by infrastructural alterations. However, I suggest that the practices of friendship do offer a significant and
novel epistemological starting point to disrupt the taken-for-granted
categorical and normative ways of thinking about and theorizing the
city. By putting theory in conversation with intimate chats and informal, improvised dialogues between friends, I hope to make possible an
imagination broad enough to allow for the enmeshment of experiences
to be taken seriously. How the doing and making of friendship are
enacted is a question that is also about how space is lived and how time
is experienced. Thus, the intimacy of friendship in this light constitutes
a "knot" between human beings as well as an enmeshment of different
analytical concepts.

Nadia

My friendship with Nadia evolved and grew as we grew older, I in
Cairo and she in Alexandria. Since 2014, we have become closer, and
our friendship has grown in a way that continues to astonish me. At the
beginning it was like discovering a new species of a plant, one that you
do not know exactly how to cultivate. There is guide for how to conduct
a friendship "comme il faut." With Nadia, the bud of our friendship

bloomed, not without effort, but it seemed that our modes of experimentation with intimacy worked well together. We stayed in touch via
the internet, and we managed to meet for a few hours whenever I visited
Alexandria, which was around three times a year. She does not come to
Cairo, because of the demanding nature of her medical studies. Also, she
lives in a strict and "conservative" household, by her own description,
and her parents are not exactly fond of the idea of her traveling alone
or with friends to Cairo. On the other hand, I visit Alexandria very
often. My mother does not mind me going on solo trips out of town,
especially to Alexandria, since she had taught me to know and love it
from a young age. My mother attended college in Alexandria, and lived
for four years in a Catholic ladies-only student dormitory building near
the University of Alexandria. Time and again, she has told me dozens
of stories about that experience, about the friends she made and the
city of Alexandria with which she built a relationship during that time.
I started to sense that there is "an Alexandria" that my mother knows
and remembers, streets that she walked, friends that she made, and a
particular configuration of the city that she had established during the
four years she lived there (from 1972 to 1976). Her Alexandria is quite
different from mine; even our desire for the city is different. I long for
an "Alexandria affect" that I cannot quite articulate, or even completely
understand. There is certainly an element of mystique or an allure in
particular places, one that cannot be accounted for by specific causes.

Between my mother, my Alexandrian friends, and myself, a particular "city affect" was being assembled for me. Stories about being inside
Alexandria, about "having been" in Alexandria, about moving between
Cairo and Alexandria kept echoing inside my head, forming something
that is not easy to label. I knew it was there, I believed Alexandria as a
place had a certain affective power over me as well as over other people,
but the "city affect" is a web of interwoven sentiments and ideas, none
of which is more dominant than the others. It is an affect that is both
specific and common. It is specific in the sense that our affective relations to the cities are formed through the personal range of experiences
that one goes through always individually, yet also always in relation
to something: people, places, objects, tastes, smells, sounds. Ultimately,
each one of us has their own unique experience of the city, and hence
their own affective relation to it. Yet the ways in which the city is said

to engender common experiences of affective urbanism are connected mainly with the ways in which the city is shared between us.

> *Urban political subjectivity thus comprises an articulated, relational assemblage. This assemblage consists of singular subjects comprising hybrid articulations of human and nonhuman material. These singular subjects are exposed to each other at the boundaries where they meet—the objects around and through which they live their lives. Urbanised political subjectivity thus consists less of citizens and their communities than singularities—the materialities they incorporate and the others to whom they are exposed. Much of this exposure happens precisely at the material surfaces that make up the things between us in the contemporary city. Walls, houses, trains, and fibers are all things that lie between us, things that might be incorporated into many different singular assemblages—and thus, as shared entities, the things that remind us of the presence of a plural alterity in the city. Thus it is the things of the city—the stone, glass, concrete, wire— which are between us in the contemporary city. . . . where walls tell us about the singularity we are when we dwell in a particular house, or wires expose us to the plural others whose messages are carried along them.* (Coward 2012:478–479)

Sometimes this "shared entity" is the water dripping from the loud air conditioners, or the water dripping from the hanging clothes on the wires above us; sometimes it is the pond that forms out of a sewer blockage or flooding in the street; everyone finds a way around them. Sometimes we stop talking because we can't scream as loudly as the surrounding car horns and police sirens. Sometimes the waiter comes in to politely imply that we need to order something to eat or to drink. He or she makes it seem as if it is a choice we can make, but it's not, really. Other times we are interrupted by kids playing a serious football match, a woman, a man, a child asking for money, selling roses, tiny brochures of Quran verses, our ringing phones, calls, texts, Facebook messages, WhatsApp messages, bumping into people we know: "Such a small world," we say. Sometimes we stop to take a picture of something we see, of ourselves, of each other. Sometimes it is an accident that has nothing to do with us, yet we stop and stare. "Something throws itself together in a moment as an event and a sensation," whispers Kathleen Stewart (2007:1). We are together, and we are together suspended in the staring and wondering, in the "where this might go," "how this will turn out"; we are suspended in the not knowing, the state of potentiality, the reverberation, the resonance, the drifting into something outside us, inside us, between us. In Alexandria's downtown, exactly like in Cairo, it is almost impossible to have an uninterrupted walk for more than 15 minutes. I am not talking about the quiet neighborhoods, the side streets, or the gated compounds with special lanes for walking and cycling, I am talking about the buzzing, pulsing, vibrating, living streets of the city that constantly act and interact with the walkers and passersby. How much they take and how much they give is never a fixed equation, but varies tremendously from one day to the next. Even if you repeat the same exact walk every day, in terms of route, you might very well be faced with a completely different experience. Similarly, our talks, our feelings, and our experiences are always liable to disruption from the "outside."

Urban Intimacy and Talking about Cities: Recuperation, Remembrances, Recompositions

> *When a rise in the sense of a shared collective atmosphere results from an occurrence, feeling historical may rhyme with feeling historic. But what we're witnessing here is what happens when a situation opens out problems in how to live that reveal a loss of trust in the historical future, threats to the sense of ongoingness in the durational present, and increased opacity within ordinary life. Life itself does not provide a ground for trust or solidarity but the sense of a shared affective management crisis does confirm belonging to a disturbed field, rather than a normative world.* (Berlant 2008b:5)

Contemplating the lived experience of cities through friendship/friends, as I walked the streets of Alexandria, I decided to have a conversation with Nadia about it. The aim was to spontaneously exchange our ideas about our home cities, how we imagine them, how we conceptualize them, and whether our friendship (or other friendships in our lives) has contributed to those imaginaries in any way. I wanted to try to think about those questions together, loosely yet in depth. By that, I mean I had not prepared any formal sets of questions or conversation starters, yet our every experience of walking the streets of downtown Alexandria together seemed like a beginning to something; it brought something up to the surface. During those walks things always happened around us and between us. Sometimes she would throw in historical information about streets, squares, closed shops, and vintage abandoned film theaters, old cinematic-looking motels, the breathtakingly beautiful churches, the semi-demolished buildings, the restaurants, the debris. Sometimes it seemed as if Nadia felt a certain duty to enlighten me about what this "is" and also what it "used to be," a transmission of something she had lived through while I had not, or had experienced at a distance. The changes in Alexandria seemed to ignite a noticeable sense of indebtedness or obligation in its people to pass on stories about it. Those stories are never free of the teller's own inevitable involvement with the places at different stages of its lifetime and different phases of its being. Here the life history of the person is enmeshed with the life history of the place. The stories of the places were never free of Nadia's own accounts of her own life and self.

Sometimes I would notice and be annoyed by the anthropologist in me imposing, if not fetishizing, certain generalities and expectations about how an "Alexandrian" sees and thinks of Alexandria and Cairo. For example, I remember how eager I was to hear what Nadia had to say about the Sidi Gaber bridge that was constructed by the Egyptian military in the summer of 2017, and how much it affected her daily routine, both while it was under construction and after it became a reality. Below is a fragment of our chat on the subject.

"Let's think together; I'll think out loud with you,' I started our chat. Nadia is not her real name, but the name she chooses to use. She was born in June 1993 into a middle-class family and has lived her whole life in Alexandria. She has three sisters; she is the eldest. After high school she entered the Faculty of Medicine in Alexandria University and at the time we had our chat she had just graduated with good grades and was about to start her obligatory one-year medical internship. Knowing her ambition for moving to Cairo, I began our chat first by lighting a cigarette, then by asking the question: "Why Cairo?" Then I noticed the correlation with Youssef Chahine's film title *Eskenderiyya leih?* but reversed, and made a brief joke about it before Nadia had the chance to respond.

N: Partially it has to do with breaking free from the constrictions of my family home. But also, the centrality, you know? The capital. I feel that there are many more things (options) there to do than here. It's like how people from other cities like Kafr al-Sheikh, al-Beheira, come to Alexandria because they feel there are more things to be done here. By things I mean everything, more and other people to meet, networks and friends to make, more work opportunities. There are lots of things happening. It's fun [in Cairo]. Here [in Alexandria] there isn't a nightlife, there's not the option of a night club. I know I wouldn't have gone every night, due to my family restrictions or finances or otherwise, but it's about having the possibility at hand. Here there isn't even that possibility. Here I'm always feeling like I'm missing out on something.

S: If it weren't for the family restrictions, would that still be the case, do you think?

N: I think it would have been different. I mean, I think the urge to go to Cairo would have been less. Or perhaps because it's something that I've wanted so bad and never happened, so the accumulation of this desire created a bigger fantasy about the possibility of being there. I think in that case I would have wanted to just visit Cairo every now and then, casually. Maybe it's not really that wonderful, perhaps it's just attached to an imagination that in real life might not be true. I love Alexandria, truly, and I don't think I want to leave it for any reason other than escaping the limitations of the family life. I have loved Alexandria since I was a kid, I love the streets and I love it.

S: But the changes that have been happening in Alex, how do you feel about that?

N: For example, while the military was building the new the Sidi Gaber bridge [2017] we lived a very difficult time during, and because of, its construction. The entire city of Alexandria was jammed. You know how Alexandria has got only two main parallel streets, the corniche road and the parallel tram one. So the roads were shifted and everyone took the narrow side streets, which are quite tiny and cannot *handle this amount of cars. I heard a story, and I'm not sure it's true, that on one of those side streets (I think Port Said Street), the ground cracked because of the car load, can you imagine? It was really a difficult time. It took us much more time than usual to reach our homes and every day it was a struggle to move from one area to another inside the city. If we were located before Sidi Gaber we had to meet there, if we were located after it, we had to meet there, but there was no way to cross that mess in order to meet. If you are in downtown, for example, and I'm in Stanley, then we can't meet, shouldn't, mustn't. This bridge (*kobri*) still feels strange, whenever I cross it I still feel a strangeness, an alienation. I feel it's temporary. Why am I seeing the sea from above like that? It looks ugly, it looks stupid.*

S: Do you think it's because it's new? What about the places that used to be there and you used to meet friends in, and then they got demolished? I mean, I hear a lot about the enforced shutting down of certain social hubs, say cultural centers, cafés, restaurants?

N: There's one café (Crystal), it's wooden and very old, and it always hosted a vast diversity of people, old and young generations. Inside it's all mirrors. They say it's going to be demolished but it's still there. People are talking about it, but I can't remember particular places that have been demolished that I was attached to and feeling miserable because of that. It's more about the change of places and the friend groups. I used to meet certain people in certain places, then the place would be taken over by a different kind of people, for example very young and loud teenagers, so we would stop going there because we were not as comfortable. The setting changes. Like there are some ahwas *[cafés] we used to go to, then at some point we started feeling we were being watched and listened to by some old men, perhaps* mokhberein *(police detectives). Speaking about whatever we wanted became less possible. Also they started forbidding large numbers of people to sit together at the same table (not more than 5). In such cases we become less comfortable and we eventually stop going. So the place might still be there but we wouldn't want to go. The cultural scene also is closing down badly (for example, Cinema Rio rooftop). They don't all close up, but some of them are prohibited*

*from hosting parties or big events, and now the scene is mostly lim-
ited to the Bibliotheca Alexandrina. The events that took place were
not all of a politically controversial or provocative nature even, in
any way, but still they are not happening any more.*

In friendship talks, the story always begins in the middle and then goes
in all directions, "perceiving, and/or making constellations of mutually
referential elements" (Guyer 2017:84). A few weeks after my conversation with Nadia, as I listened to the recording, I realized that we
zigzagged from Cairo to Alexandria, then forward, backward, and side-
ways to other things too. What was most interesting and vivid was the
way the fluidity of movement-in-thought between friends allows for a
more layered and more wide-ranging exploration of "big," "classic," or
"hegemonic," analytical themes like making sense of "place," re-telling
"memory," understanding "belonging," or even the "bridge moment" as a
somewhat politically burdened and quietly violent occurrence. Intimacy
started to resemble calm seas, where whatever was deeply submerged
had a chance, not matter how briefly, to rise to the surface. It was precisely in those moments that I had the most difficult and burdensome
sentiments of doubt about whether I would want to work on a project
that plays on the very fine line between the personal and the public,
the academic and the confessional, the spoken and and the unsaid that
friends share, all of which carry equally rich accumulations of knowledge. However, I managed to learn a technique of snapping out of the
stiff and anxiety-fueled research mode and into the open fields and
folds of the trust and comfort of intimacy. The project ran mainly on
a sense of trust in the value, the vibrancy, and the richness of the bond
of friendship and the talks between friends. By that I mean that there
is something significant and worth knowing engraved deep in the talks
and walks that friends do together.

*Understanding friendships within the context of urban encounter is
about relationships enacted in a particular time-space.* (Kathiravelu
2013:10)

When our conversation first began, I initially had a curious thought,
a vague idea about friendships and cities, that I wanted to think

through and learn more about with Nadia. I have known, throughout our four-year friendship, that she is fascinated by (the thought of) Cairo, and this is what at first seemed like an important question to ask. What was striking in Nadia's response was not only what she said, but also what she did not—more precisely, what she did not need to say to me. It quickly became clear that what she says to me, as well as the ways in which I take in Nadia's words, will always be heavily influenced by what I already know about her. To be more clear, I knew for a fact that Nadia had always wanted to go to Cairo, and that she had certain visions and expectations about what Cairo, the capital, the big city, would offer her. In fact, I have a reservoir of sometimes contradictory narratives from my Alexandrian friends about how they perceive Cairo, whether at a distance or through real-life experiences. However, I wanted to be able to pay careful attention to the ways in which each friend's experience or story needs to be illuminated using the details of their own lives, while also acknowledging the hegemony of the larger and somewhat dominant "Cairo imaginary" that resonates among so many people. Nadia, like some of my other friends, retains a particular imagination of Cairo that screams possibility, surprise, potential. Once another Alexandrian friend, Jihan, described it to me as: "Alexandria now feels like a glass box. I know everything and everyone; there are no chances for anything new and exciting to happen." Jihan's statement strongly echoed the sentiments of Nadia and other Alexandrian friends. Nadia herself spoke bluntly about her "fetish" of the capital city, which she knows might not actually be real. Rather than building up to an absolute, final narrative about Cairo, I wanted to know where Nadia's narrative came from and how it developed. We ended up talking about her family, their extremely religious background, the strict and inflexible obligations they impose on her. A few of the things we talked about were the medical school, her love life, her two best friends, the quality and quantity of social circles and networks that surround her, her future ambitions, Alexandria and its narrow streets, Cairo and its heavy traffic, the limited cultural scene in Alexandria, and the political anxiety around public artistic performances. My point is that there was no limit to how far we could go, together and unguided, to events, moments, and places in our lives that evoked notions of time and space, how they are lived and made sense of. We were able to trace each question, thought, and assumption back, freely, to all of its associations. The trust and mutual understanding that our friendship had granted us permitted a unique depth and an exceptional generosity in our intellectual exploration.

In "Thinking about Feeling Historical" (2008b), Lauren Berlant examines the several affective genres, registers, and atmospheres of how the historical present moment is apprehended, sensed, lived, and articulated. She attempts to "rethink the sensing of history, and of the historic" (Berlant 2008b:4). Berlant points out that the processes of sense-making across multiple affective registers generate a sense of shared affective management that involves reassessing the conditions of ongoingness, in focused and unfocused ways, and "produces a way of grasping and inhabiting a collectively significant 'unthought known'" (Berlant 2008b:7). Old landscapes, changed streets, and new infrastructures create a moment of shared absorbing and making sense of what is here, now. As Berlant writes:

> *Meeting the present is like meeting a new lover: telling the story of how you got to be this way in the present moment suddenly changes its usual cadences because of the occasion of the telling. Where you are from is suddenly a different "somewhere" else, underdescribed or even hidden by the idiom of nation or state: the state's name becomes a ridiculous sound that reminds you of where you were ridiculous and unsound. It is a handle on something historical barely yet experienced. It used to matter, where you came from, because you felt akin to the other people who lived there, since they knew what you knew—the landscape that the highway skims and random facts associated with patriotism. But now the enmeshing of global power and ordinary life has turned the scenic route into a situation.* (2008b:9)

In the acts of telling, hearing, remembering, looking around, pointing to things, wondering, and asking questions, cities are made and remade between people. Drawing on Berlant, there is an "us" that is constituted by the "pooling and spooling what we have seen and what we know" (Berlant 2008b:9), a "we" that is made by an ongoing activity of "catching up" with life as it is happening. Friendship practiced within an urban intimate context thus involves processes of recomposition of the present moment in time as well as in space on one hand, and on the other enables the production of affective and emotional relations between friends, activating a simultaneous re-production of selves and intimacies.

Accordingly, the "affective" element of the everyday enactments and practices of friendship retains an extremely valuable significance and productive potential, although it has not enjoyed much academic attention. In this light, and following Lavaanya Kathiravelu (2013), friendship as a form of social relation and interaction must be examined in conjunction with understandings of diverse urban settings. In other words, the literature on human geographies and politics of spatiality must be brought together with intimate and thick ethnographic research on social and affective configurations of "relationships, networks and ties built on trust, respect and reciprocity" (Kathiravelu 2013:3). Kathiravelu's paper calls for a rather thicker mode of examining the affective bonds of friendship between different as well as similar urban residents, which is something I have attempted to do in the course of the fieldwork for this chapter. I believe that examining a particular personal friendship of mine with a person from a different city under this light offers novel ways of understanding urban politics of companionship and coexistence. Such ethnographic attunement pushes the boundaries of academic inquiry, and stretches to take in the urban dwellers' own articulations of their social, spatial, and temporal experiences, in their own languages of expression. "Friendships, in this sense, are seen as tangible ways in which the larger 'urban unconscious' can be felt, linking the intimate sphere of private lives and relationships with a public urban commons" (Kathiravelu 2013:3).

Here, friendship as an analytic framework can work dually. On the one hand, friendship talks hold reservoirs of constructions of place, whether imagined or lived, that perpetuate themselves along the lines of the relationship itself. Friends keep going back to the same place, but it is never the same, and it is their friendship that bears the change and that enables new ways of sense-making and potential re-enactments, re-engagements, or different attachments to take place. On the other hand, friendship talks also serve, metaphorically, as a place that friends can always go back to—meaning that, as much as it contains potential for movement further in time, it also enables a particular reassemblage of elements in order to "catch up with" a place that is no longer the same, for the sake of carving a moment in the present where friends can stand still, rest, and dwell.

In the above section of the chapter I have engaged with the deep, personal, and inspiring ethnographic talks and walks that I had with Nadia, and what came out of them. My friendship with Nadia contains a particular Alexandria, the Alexandria I know. The places we repeatedly go, the encounters that unfold in them, the stories that she narrates to me about them, together form a unique map for navigating the city, one that will always be tied to this specific relationship, its history, and its potential ongoingness. Nadia's intimate and open talk with me disrupted and suspended a certain fetishistic question that I began my fieldwork with, and pushed me to a different level of analysis. The question was something like "How does the disappearance of public places and infrastructures where friends met and gathered affect the social bond between friends themselves? Do friendships dissolve more easily with the fast-paced urban alterations that are now happening in cities like Cairo and Alexandria?" Paying close attention to my conversations with Nadia and my other friends, both Alexandrian and Cairene, it began to be clear to me that the subjects' configurations of spatiality spread well beyond the narrow dimensions of such a question. Places are important, but the happenings that unfolded in them do not vanish with their disappearance. In other words, my friends have told me that the absence of places does not take away the togetherness of friends. It is still up to them to be(come) together through the loss of the old and the birth of the new. Friends carry between them a map that traces a history of companionship that transverses the 'too much abstraction' of categories and the 'too much concreteness' of the violent reshaping of cities. Nadia is constitutive of the Alexandria I know and happen to have an emotional attachment to, by virtue of what our friendship gave me in and about that place, over a period of time.

The ultimate aim of a politics of worldbuilding, then, is the actual building of new worlds, including not only their infrastructure, values, and interactive practices, but, first and foremost, the onto-ethical grounds that allow for such worlds to emerge and remain. These are relationalities of being-with that onto-ethically sustain new possibilities for a community of whoever arrives, freedom as letting-be, and attuned care. A politics of worldbuilding as agonistic experimentation with an otherwise entails actually enacting this otherwise so that it begins to stick and endure, rather than dissipate as if it never was. (Zigon 2017)

In Friendship We Dwell: On Movement and Stillness

> *People pray to each other. The way I say "you" to someone else, respectfully, intimately, desperately. The way someone says "you" to me, hopefully, expectantly, intensely . . .*
> —Huub Oosterhuis

You   who I don't know   I don't know how to talk to you

—What is it like for you there?

Here . . . well, wanting solitude; and talk; friendship—
The uses of solitude. To imagine; to hear.
Learning braille. To imagine other solitudes.
But they will not be mine;
to wait, in the quiet; not to scatter the voices—
What are you afraid of?

What will happen. All this leaving. And meetings, yes. But death.
What happens when you die?

". . . not scatter the voices,"

Drown out. Not make a house, out of my own words. To be quiet in another throat; other eyes; listen for what it is like there. What word. What silence. Allowing. Uncertain: to drift, in the restlessness . . . Repose. To run like water—

What is it like there, right now?

Listen: the crowding of the street; the room. Everyone hunches in against the crowding; holding their breath: against dread.

What do you dread?

What happens when you die?
What do you dread, in this room, now?

Not listening. Now. Not watching. Safe inside my own skin.
To die, not having listened. Not having asked . . . To have scattered
life.

Yes I know: the thread you have to keep finding, over again, to follow
it back to life; I know. Impossible, sometimes. (Valentine 2004)

The word "Me" is felt only in the warmth of the group, like when you
knock on the door of those you love and they ask, "Who?" and you say,
"Me," and they know you by the tone of your voice. (Haddad 2012,
my translation)

In the Arabic version of his poem, Fouad Haddad uses *hessak*, which
can be translated as "the tone of your voice" but also as "the affect of
your being." *Hess* in its literal sense is translated as someone's voice, but
also quite commonly as a metaphor for the unique affective presence
of an individual, the very special value and the preciousness it brings.
Haddad's poetic phrase seizes a certain response that is revealing of a
deep familiarity and recognition. They know you, even though you have
only uttered "me" and not your name; they know you because they know
something of your presence that goes beyond your name; they recognize you before you even demand recognition. They have an affective
relation to you that is not reducible to the normative manners in which
people identify themselves and claim acknowledgment in the world.
They know the tone of your voice, perhaps also the sound of your foot-
steps, their very particular pace.

Building on and responding to the first part of this chapter, I now
wish to discuss three practices of friendship that will help concret-
ize and make visible the links between friendship and movement,
friendship and rest, and whether friendship can be theorized as a
space where friends mutually dwell. The notion of "dwelling" here is a

concept traced along lines drawn first by Martin Heidegger, and after him Tim Ingold. We do know that "dwelling" is the "inhabiting" of and "residing" in the world. We know that Heidegger succeeded in pushing the boundaries of the term, from being strictly tied to notions of residence to encompassing the polymorphous ways in which one lives one's life. Building is not a prerequisite for dwelling, but dwelling comes first for Heidegger, because human beings need to first situate themselves within their surroundings: the sky, the rain, the sunshine, the ground. The essence of life, to Heidegger, is a fundamental mode of dwelling, which is "not the occupation of a world already built, but the very process of inhabiting the earth" (Ingold 2011:147), and this necessarily comes before any kind of building can begin to take place. Ingold pushes the notion of dwelling even further to include the various forms of life that humans work with, whether in the imagination or in reality, to produce and bear meaning within the moving and changing currents of their lifeworlds. To Ingold, dwelling is about the "immersion" of beings in life, singly and together, or the ways in which they deploy their capacities of attention and response in their practices and experience. Dwelling here is intimately tied with movement, as Ingold suggests that the essence of what it means to dwell is "to be embarked upon a movement along a way of life . . . The path, and not the place, is the primary condition of being, or rather of becoming" (Ingold 2011:12).

Working with what both Heidegger and Ingold present, and extending the realm of how dwelling might be imagined and theorized, I would like to add that it is also an act of creating a "footing"[7] in the world by means of cultivating a shared promise of intimacy, like a place one can go back to, rest in, and then move forward from. Here friendship, even if momentarily, acts as a space of mutual dwelling offering a respite or refuge from a world of instability, discontinuity, and uncertainty while mediating its vastness.

Witness(ing).

The presence of others who see what we see and hear what we hear assures us of the reality of the world and ourselves. (Arendt 1998:50)

---

7   A term borrowed from Lauren Berlant (2016).

Bearing witness is an active and ongoing act of being "there," taking an actual part of the life of the friend, whether closely or at a distance. Friends witness the changes and flows in each other's lives as well as the currents and tides of their surrounding environment. The presence of another who sees what we see and hears what we hear, as Hannah Arendt beautifully writes in *The Human Condition*, creates a particular grounding, as I have mentioned earlier, a footing that is found in the shared encounter of intimacy yet not necessarily tied to consistency or continuity in the surrounding physical and infrastructural environment. "Witnessing" here is not defined as a mere collective "watching," "seeing," or passively "staring" at what is out there as it changes and becomes otherwise. Instead, it is an active responding to the life of the other as it unfolds. At the same time, friends witness together the unmaking and remaking of the physical spaces they inhabit; this involves multiple sequences of negotiations and questions about what to hold on to and what to let go of, and how. In dynamic cities like those of the Global South in particular, where change is extremely fast paced, we preserve perceptions of and attachments to places in the stories that we share. When the place becomes otherwise, part of the story remains in the accumulated knowledge between friends, in talks or experiences, and hence the place never totally disappears since another has witnessed it in the same way as I did. The ability to exercise witnessing as a form of care creates a shared horizon of meaning and understanding rooted in their togetherness.

Catching up.

> For if remembering does not make the past into an object, then nor does imagining make an object of the future. That is to say, to imagine is not to project the future, as a state of affairs distinct from the present. It is rather to catch a life that, in its hopes and dreams, has a way of running ahead of its moorings in the material world. Where it runs is beyond the horizon of our conceptualization. At this horizon, future and past are no longer distinguishable. They merge at the ends of longing, in a place where all imagining is remembering, and all remembering imagining. It is a place we perpetually dream of and strive for, but never reach. (Ingold 2017b:13)

Catching up with friends can be seen as a mode of slow affective and attentive activity of "presencing," a term coined by Ingold, which means an activity capable of bringing together past remembering and future imagining in the active act of telling in the here and now. Catching up occurs as a movement that happens in time but that also takes place in actual built environment or spaces, acting as an invitation to trust and an enactment of responsiveness. It is a kind of "telling" that reproduces spatial and temporal contexts of a past moment, planting them in a field of trust that is the friend. This kind of telling is different, as Todd May had previously argued, from acts of "saying," "asserting," or putting claims out to the public as an individual occupying the same space and adding to the general stock of knowledge. Catching up is an excellent example of what Ingold describes as correspondence of lives: "In answering to one another, lifelines co-respond," implying a necessary fluidity and resonance with the movement of the things to which it attends. He writes, "that awareness is always awareness with before it is ever awareness of. We can recognize a movement, and respond to it, before we ever fix it in our sights" (Ingold 2017b:12).

Catching up between friends over time is an emergent symbolic picking up of pieces or fragments of life as-it-unfolds. In the simple acts of listening, paying attention, and following the life of the friend, what seem like ordinary everyday practices become non-authoritarian and non-deterministic registers or resources that hold the possibility of preservation, recuperation, and redemption. Building on Jane I. Guyer (2017), in those "ordinary practices" of sharing stories, every word that is uttered and every story shared becomes part of a larger assemblage or collective archive of knowledge for ongoing life. The radicality of this archive of intimacy, companionship, and coexistence lies in the rhythmic worlding it performs, each time friends take the time to do it. They recompose pasts and imagine futures to come, while strengthening the tie that binds them to each other and to the world. This archive pushes forth a possibility of reinhabiting the present differently, "as it pulls us off the center of ourselves, allowing us to expend ourselves on behalf of the friend" (May 2012:80). Using small elements of continuing value from yesterday and recombining them in meaningful ways with new elements from today and tomorrow (Guyer 2017), one can compose alternative approaches to emergent yet unknown futures in specific times and places.

Staying in touch/synch.

> *Living compassionately, sharing in the suffering of the other, does not*
> *require anything like complete understanding (and might, in fact,*
> *necessitate the disruption of this very yearning). Rather, living com-*
> *passionately requires recognizing and facing our responsibility to the*
> *infinitude of the other, welcoming the stranger whose very existence is the*
> *possibility of touching and being touched, who gifts us with both the abil-*
> *ity to respond and the longing for justice-to-come.* (Barad 2012:219)

During Ramadan 2012, a very famous television commercial came out
and immediately became the hit of the year. It was a four-minute song
filmed in different cities in Egypt (Cairo, Alexandria, Aswan, Port Said)
about different modes of solidarity between people for the larger cause,
being a part of the solid Egyptian nation. The scenes included people
sitting together in public cafés, fans at a football match, families at a
rural wedding, Bedouins, *saʿidis* (people from rural upper Egypt). The
introduction of the song goes as follows:

> *For we have got to be together*
> *For we share the same land*
> *For tomorrow, which awaits*
> *And does not want to break us apart.*

The song attempted to produce a simplistic and light-hearted narrative about the integrity, the distinctive nature of the "Egyptian" citizen.
The commercial illustrates the powerful solidarity that characterizes
the nation, acting as a safeguard to each good and caring citizen, of
whom we see dozens on screen throughout the commercial. Artistic
as it was, the song resembled a national anthem in the ways in which
it conformed to a monolithic singular narrative about patriotic love for
the country and the necessary fraternal harmony among its citizens.
Friendship was mentioned a couple of times in the song, promoted as
the ideal social bond that strengthens, supports, and pushes the collective forward, while also fostering the hope that stability will follow
if everyone works together. However, as we have previously discussed,
living in a constantly shifting environment requires a recasting of the

social life in a way that is open to improvisation, not a reliance on specific and positive projections into the future.

As Brian Massumi argues in his latest book, *The Principle of Unrest: Activist Philosophy in the Expanded Field* (2017), the obsession of the macro-political involves thinking in terms of structured, bounded "wholes" or "unities." The macro-political cannot function without inscribing boundaries that delineate criteria for eligibilities. In order to include, they also have to exclude, and this mode of organization (imposed from above) is fundamental to how the macro-political state defines the notion of the social field. This is similar to what AbdouMaliq Simone proposes in his article "Passing Things Along: (In)completing Infrastructure" (2016) by exploring the act of making "statements" as a way of making something "known," or "visible." Whether such statements are issued by the state or the residents themselves, whether to make a claim on a space or consolidate an identity, they end up acting as contracts that frame the conditions and the capacities of persons to be part of specific kinds of places and relationships. "Statements draw lines among those considered worthy, eligible, and common, and inscribe divides among bodies and spaces. Statements are lines of delivery and articulation; they seal deals, define memberships, and incite antagonisms" (Simone 2016:152). If they define people as coherent entities to be addressed, they also define the contours of spaces in which individuals can operate. Whereas—returning to Massumi—on the micro-political level, things are very different. He writes:

> At the micropolitical level there's a multiplication of differentiations and a vagueness that's not a simple lack of definition, but an overfullness with potential. . . . There's a fringe or periphery that goes out in all directions, full of tendencies that have not been actualized, but might be at another moment, under different conditions. . . . So the micropolitical field is a constitutively open multiplicity populated by tendencies and potentials, not subjects or objects. (Massumi 2017:104)

Without having to conform to an assigned position vis-à-vis an overarching cause, within the interstices of the life of intimacy there is a lived "belief in the world" (Deleuze 1995:176). This belief is sufficient to engender "new space-times however small their surface or volume" (176). To stay-in-touch is to remain close, and I would like to add, without a mapped-out "plan." To borrow a line from Chris Marker's astounding short video essay, *2084*: "but exactly in this period of great truths, it's rather healthy to imagine other things. For example, one way of acquiring new certainties is to learn to doubt together" (Marker 1984).

In the mutual efforts for sustaining friendship in cities-in-motion, friendship manifests as a space in the public imaginary and also in our private lives that people can return to. Far from being a utopia, it can be described as a space "defined by relationality" (Berardi 2009:195), allowing "virtual co-presence of potentials" (Massumi 2015:5).

Friendship becomes a mode of practicing the ordinary, everyday, big and small ethics of re-creating a livable life, for oneself as well as for others. It is a value, a vocation, and a practice that is as much about surprise, and the emergence of flows and attachments, as it is about repetition. It is about recognizing, seeing, and containing the other without being overwhelmed by the friction, or intoxicated or destroyed by the uncertainty and fluidity of the relation. The fluidity inherent in the relationship of friendship is crucial to the making and maintaining of the bond, imbuing it with an adaptability to unknown and unknowable futures. Creating infrastructures of sociality and intimacy is necessary in order to be able to confront, handle, and perhaps challenge the top-down spatial alterations. Staying in touch can be seen as a means to build "affective infrastructures" that respond to needs and desires for a different future as they help bring them into being.

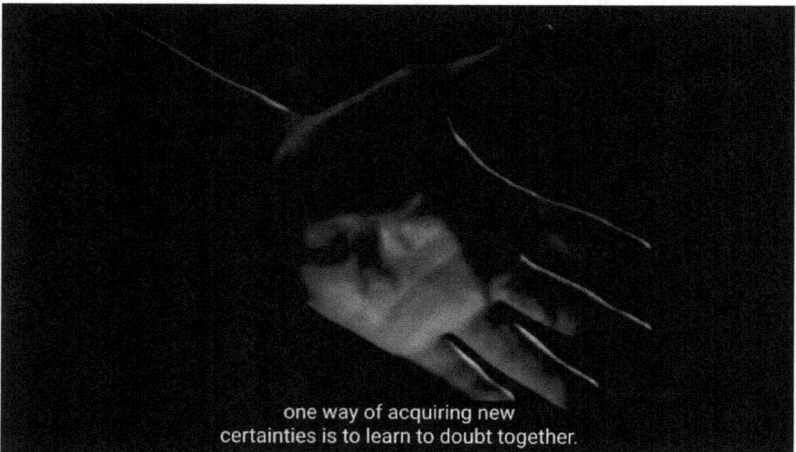

one way of acquiring new certainties is to learn to doubt together.

The goal is to make an attempt at becoming and staying in touch/ in synch, while being ready for the next phase of movement. Reclaiming the space through and by and within friendship happens in the social proximity of friends that hold outs the prospect of a world worth attaching to, one "that's something other than an old hope's bitter echo" (Berlant 2016). Here, the infrastructure of the social or friendship emerges and takes on the dynamics of an open plan. That is, we need to cultivate a skill at transforming whatever separates or seeks to separate, in order to make it a space where we can connect. This effort can be applied both spatially, converting spaces from the capitalist sanitary alienating zones to zones of shared encounters, and temporally, as the common memories and repetitive encounters offer the ground for a relationship embedded in similar habits or values.

"Where is the friend's house?"
Horseman asked by twilight and
The sky paused.

The passerby presented sands, the branch of light that he had
in mouth
And pointed to a poplar tree and said:

"Before reaching the tree,
There is a garden alley that is greener than God's sleep
And in it, love is as blue as the feathers of honesty.
Go to the end of the alley which stops at the back of adolescence.
Then turn to the flower of loneliness.
Two steps short of reaching the flower,
Stay by the fountain of eternal myth of earth
And you feel a transparent fear.
And in the fluid sincerity of the air, you will hear a scratch:
You will see a child
Who has gone up the pine tree, to grab a bird from the nest of light
And you ask him
Where the friend's house is."
Sohrab Sepehri (1988), translated by Mahvash Shahegh

CHAPTER 4

That It Is from Your Eye that I Find Myself: The Making of Friendship, the Making of Selves

Brown: So friendship is the soil out of which one has to walk in the larger world.

Illich: I wish it were the soil. I wish there were still soil to it. And it is not friendship unless there is something a little bit dirty to it. Dirty you don't say in English. You know, dirt in the good sense. Earthy.

Brown: Fleshy.

Illich: Because the eyes are fleshy. That image in there, in your pupilla, of me is fleshy. (Illich and Brown 1996)

> *I know another person's thought*
> *and who I am, I know that not.*
> *My vision is too close to me—*
> *I am not what I saw and see.*
> *I'd use myself more perfectly*
> *if I could move away from me.*
> *Yet not so distant as my foe!*
> *My closest friend's too far off, no—*
> *give me instead the middle ground!*
> *Do you surmise what I propound?* (Nietzsche 2001:15–16)

In this chapter I am interested in exploring the cracks within friendship, the precise moments where each friend is opened up, made vulnerable by the revelations that emerge in the encounter of friendship, or rather in the ruptures of friendship. By drawing on ethnographic material, art-work in the Egyptian media, and the existing literature on friendship, I wish to explore the simultaneous making and breaking of notions of the self when challenged or confused by the intimacy shared between two or more friends. How do our friends contribute to the processes of reassessing one's own self, and to the reconfiguring of one's own view of oneself? Do our friends make us see ourselves better or differently? What transformative potential does friendship have, in terms of one's character? Historically, conceptions and imaginaries around the "good" person assume that s/he will make a "good" friend. I am interested in how those links are made and unmade in the life experiences of making and losing friends. I argue that those assumptions about the goodness of a person forming the standard of what constitutes a good friend no longer hold, because intimacy entails a set of complicated ventures, interactions, and intersubjectivities, processes of growth and decay, that constantly rework and reconfigure the definitions of and the binaries between the self and the other—in this case, the friend.

By drawing on a fictional female friendship depicted in an Egyptian film made in 2005 and male friendship in a prominent Egyptian television series broadcast during Ramadan 2017, I will explore how friends were depicted and what aspects of the relationship of friend-ship were highlighted and mobilized. Inspired by Lauren Berlant, I believe that artworks in mass media—films, television ads, or television series—can be important sites for tracking "repetitions": gestures and scenes of the present as a "mediated affect" (Berlant 2011a:4). I found Berlant's methodology of reading and tracking patterns and repetitions across different aesthetic and social contexts useful in identifying the ways in which the affective expressions that appear in contemporary art works both embed and express "structures of feeling" (see Williams and Orrom 1954; Williams 1977) that are central to the conceptualization of everyday life and the pressures of the present moment on "the subject's sensorium" (Berlant 2011a:9). Berlant notes how literary or cinematic moments can give voice to particular "organized but unspoken" arrange-ments of experience, "a residue of common historical experience sensed but not spoken in a social formation" (Berlant 2011a:65). I argue that the depiction of the figure of the "friend" in the public media is in many ways becoming more and more expressive of the imperfect and flawed nature of friendship, loosening the grip of the static classifications of what constitutes a "good" or a "bad" friend. The two art works I have chosen revolve around the lives of two or more friends, though the works themselves are not typically about friendship. Instead, they follow friends as life happens to them, as individuals and also as a group. Combining these works with ethnographic fragments, I aim to trace how the bond of friendship can be extended beyond the ancient Greek concept of "philos." I will make use of the terms Deleuze uses in his philosophical engagement with friendship (1991) and in his correspondence with Dionys Mascolo on the theme of friendship (Deleueze 2006): "distress," "amnesia," and "aphasia."

On Naked Personalities and Difficult Truths

Unless we are led back to the "Friend," but after an ordeal that is too powerful, an inexpressible catastrophe, and so in yet another new sense, in a mutual distress, a mutual weariness that forms a new right of thought (Socrates becomes Jewish). Not two friends who communicate and recall the past together but, on the contrary, who suffer an amnesia or aphasia capable of splitting thought, of dividing it in itself. Personae proliferate and branch off, jostle one another and replace each other. (Deleuze and Guattari 1994:71)

When someone's eyes turn to me, it is other light sources they seek, glowing in the light, to extend the depth of light in which he or she circulates. Sometimes, to be sure, the other looks to me to receive from me the image of what my eyes have seen; the other I meet on the Himalayan trek asks of me if I have seen the path to the grand visions that eyes are made to see. (Lingis 1994:214)

The famous novelist, poet, literary critic, and academic C. S. Lewis wrote a short but significant essay that appeared in the collection *Friendship: A Philosophical Reader* published in 1993, entitled "Friendship: The Least Necessary Love." The essay is an excerpt from his longer and more detailed discussion of friendship in his book *The Four Loves* (1960). The essay's title captures one of Lewis's main arguments, which is that friendship is not a love based on or driven by biological instincts: "there is nothing throaty about it; nothing that quickens the pulse or turns you red and pale" (Lewis 1993:40). Lewis describes the affection that comes with and from friendship as tranquil, unlike "Eros"; it does not quicken the heart or rack the nerves or charge one's brain with negative or consuming intensity. Unlike lovers who stand face to face, friends, in Lewis's eyes, stand side by side in a scene of proximity. A friend is neither jealous nor needy; it is a relationship of "disentangled, or stripped minds . . . naked personalities" (44). From this understanding springs the question: "'Do you see the same truth?' Or at least, 'Do you care about the same truth?'" (42). Lewis proposes that the birth of friendship takes place at the moment "when one man says to another 'what? You too? I thought I was the only one'" (42). This is, in other words, a moment of revelation of a certain commonness that breaks the isolation, the estrangement, of singularity. He writes, "Friendship arises out of mere Companionship when two or more of the companions discover that they have in common some insight or interest or even taste which the others do not share and which, till that moment, each believed to be his own unique treasure (or burden)" (41–42). Yet this experience of commonness that initially brings two or more persons together may and most probably does fade over time, and although friends need to keep a balanced appreciation and admiration for one other, according to Lewis they must be careful not to become a "mutual admiration society" (47) that exists just for the sake of something that "was" in the past and no longer "is." What is problematic about Lewis's assumption is that it overlooks the complexity, irregularity, and unpredictability inherent in processes of growth and change. That is, the enchantment of the moment when we find another person who sees and cares about the same "truth" as us is a brief occurrence that either develops into friendship—which in its turn will not be free of interruptions, disagreements, and divergences—or will wither with the withering of the initial incident or impulse of commonality. As we grow up, there is an inevitability to the changes that occur inside as well as outside us. While some experiences may preserve their shape, others fade or become less relevant. Also, there is nothing fixed or naturally forever about the particular traits, tendencies, characteristics, attitudes, and beliefs that we acquire at a young age. The unpredictability of life runs parallel to the unpredictability of the personal growth of human beings, which directly affects how they see themselves and how they see others in the world, and basically shapes and reshapes the kind of friends or intimate others that they desire or imagine themselves with. Hence I would argue that the sustenance of friendship over time depends mainly on whether both friends are able and willing to re-produce themselves and re-create their friendship differently.

This least necessary love, this love between friends, is indeed non-biological and certainly not a force majeure, yet one could say that it is precisely this non-necessity that renders its creation and maintenance difficult and daring. For that reason it might be useful to bring Deleuze and Guattari into conversation with Lewis on the subject of friendship. Besides being two of the most influential philosophers of the twentieth century, Deleuze and Guattari sustained a friendship in life and in thinking (which eventually manifested itself in writing) that has continued to inspire generations of readers around the world.

In their innovative and intellectually stimulating text *What Is Philosophy?*, Deleuze and Guattari offer a fresh reconceptualization of the figure of the friend, the original ground upon which Western philosophy was first built. The task was and still is important, to evoke (and perhaps capture the failures of) the earlier political ideas of friendship understood as democratic consensus between equals, because this meaning of 'friend' at the time of the Greeks no longer designates a "living category". Deleuze and Guattari speak from a point in history where the ideal Greek vision of friendship based on equality, virtue, and clear communication had already been obscured by capitalism. Deleuze and Guattari respond to the classic Greek model of friendship in a manner that is deeper and more complex, going beyond the peaceful state of consensus and equality, introducing the implicit potentials of hostility, betrayal, distress, and distrust that exist between friends. They establish the figure of the "conceptual persona":

> *Or again, if we say that a conceptual persona is the Friend, or that he is the Judge or the Legislator, we are no longer concerned with private, public, or legal status but with that which belongs by right to thought*

and only to thought. Stammerer, friend, or judge do not lose their con-crete existence but, on the contrary, take on a new one as thought's internal conditions for its real exercise with this or that conceptual persona. This is not two friends who engage in thought; rather, it is thought itself that requires the thinker to be a friend so that thought is divided up within itself and can be exercised. It is thought itself which requires this division of thought between friends. These are no longer empirical, psychological, and social determinations, still less abstractions, but intercessors, crystals, or seeds of thought. (Deleuze and Guattari 1994:69)

The friend's presence in this view is "intrinsic to thought, a condition of possibility of thought itself, a living category, a transcendental lived reality" (3). Deleuze and Guattari thus arrive at an account of the friend as thought divided within itself, thus forming the possibility of thinking as a process or a conversation (Lambert 2008:48). Yet unlike the Greek philosophers' view, this sort of conversation is not merely around a certain "entity," an essence or an essential truth that needs to be either validated or disproved, but rather "going through trials with that person like apha-sia and amnesia that are necessary for any thinking" (Deleuze 2006:329).

A deeper investigation of Deleuze's amnesia and aphasia has been undertaken by the prominent philosopher and literary theorist Gregg Lambert. In "Deleuze and the Political Ontology of 'The Friend' (Phi-los)" (2008) Lambert traces the notion of "catastrophe" as proposed by Deleuze, as the thing that evokes and tests the concreteness of the situ-ation of friendship. This catastrophe introduces the concept of aphasia and amnesia between friends. Aphasia by definition is a communication disorder; it does not clinically impair the person's intelligence, yet it gets in the way of the person's ability to express oneself, to find the right words to say what one means. As a term used to describe a certain state within friendship, perhaps it can be metaphorically called the lag, the paralysis one feels when one cannot find a common ground with the friend upon which to speak. In Lambert's words, "Aphasia is not deter-mined here by the simple form of strife or conflict that causes silence, as when 'friends don't speak with one another,' but refers to a more fun-damental experience of the loss of a common language of friendship" (Lambert 2008:43). Of amnesia he writes,

*Amnesia must be understood as more extreme than the simple forgetful-
ness that occurs "between friends," as when they are separated by distance
or time. . . . Normal conceptions of friendship are usually bordered by these
conditions of permanence and volatility, and they are part of what distin-
guishes "the friend" from other social relationships, such as the relationship
with the stranger, the member of the family or the mere acquaintance.
(What is particular to the relationship that defines "the friend" is a character of becoming that does not seem to belong to these other relationships.)
However, the experience of real amnesia or aphasia can never be imagined to belong to friendship, unless by the intervention of some catastrophe
or by an "outside" force that first appears as violence.* (Lambert 2008:43)

Lambert sheds light on the Deleuzian engagement with the Greek
concept of friendship, and on the radical perspectives that Deleuze suggested are fundamental to thinking and theorizing about friendship.
The possibilities of betrayal and distress or the exhaustion of friendship
are things that Deleuze puts forward as integral to friendship, meaning
that the tranquil state of consensus and commonality always coexists
with the threat of an outbreak, a falling-out, a difference that it cannot
pacify or repress, or through which it cannot communicate (Lambert
2008:39). Here, the Deleuzian discourse on friendship offers a mode
for imagining the relationship beyond the narrow confines of predetermined likes and similarities as the sole basis for proximity and intimacy.

Jumana and Yasmine: We Hide and We Seek (Each Other)

Enemies can't break your spirit, only friends can. (Roy 2017b:129)

In 2005, the acclaimed Egyptian filmmaker and screenwriter Mohammed Khan made yet another film that revolves around the lifeworlds
of two friends. Khan was one of the most prominent directors in
Egypt in the 1980s. He apparently had a very particular passion for
and appreciation of friendship, always portrayed in a deeply embedded manner within the context of the larger atmosphere in which it
is practiced. One of these films is *Dreams of Hind and Camelia* (*Ahlam
Hind wa Kamilya*, Khan 1988), a poignant story of two maids in Cairo
and their common struggle in making and sustaining a life. As they

become friends, they also become each other's motivation and hope for emancipation and well-being. *Downtown Girls* (*Banat Wust al-Balad*, Khan 2005), another film by Khan, tells the story of two working-class young women who find and befriend each other in the metro in Cairo. They come from different, lower-middle-class neighborhoods in Cairo; one of them, Yasmine, works in a beauty salon, and the other, Jumana, works in a lingerie shop. Both the beauty salon and the shop lie in the downtown area of Cairo. Khan situates the story within a real mise-en-scène of the particular historical, social, cultural, and economic moment of 2005 in Cairo. Our protagonists are in their mid-twenties and full of life. Yasmine and Jumana are not crushed by the difficulties of their jobs, their households, or even their obviously long commute to and from work. Early in the film, we learn about the two women's fantasies, dreams, and personal ambitions, but also sense the tensions that are clearly entrenched in their friendship as a result of their overlapping dreams and fantasies. Yasmine and Jumana do live in relatively stable households with their families, but I describe them as "relatively stable" because they only seem "normal" from the outside. Jumana is the only member of her family still living at the family's house with the mother, who suffers from late-stage Alzheimer's and who constantly hallucinates since the death of her husband. Yasmine lives in a typical lower-middle-class Egyptian household with her mother, younger brother, and father, who is mostly away, working as a train driver. Yasmine's family is apparently happy and stable, until her father confesses to her, and only to her, that he is married to another woman and has two other children and is awaiting a new baby.

The two young women are filled with dreams of a different life. Each one dreams of the handsome, successful, and financially well-off knight in shining armor who will sweep her off her feet. Their intimacy enfolds multiple and sometimes rough and contradictory feelings for each other, at the moment when they realize the threat of the possible competition between them, or when their fantasies seem to be so identical that one of them has to let go, or step aside, for the other to win. At many moments of the film, Jumana wonders loudly, "Who do you think will get married first?" The film spotlights the everyday struggles that both women face on a daily basis, whether at home with their families, or at their workplaces with their bosses, or even in the street and the metro.

For Khan, the mundane of the everyday is everything. He reveals in full detail the emotional, psychological, and sometimes physical violence that the women are exposed to, but that they share only with each other. In those moments of relating, what the two women share are affective narratives that carry the weight of their distress, immobility, and exhaustion, and that explain why they decide to endure, or not endure, this cruel life, as the subjects themselves perceive it. Here, "ordinary becomes an archive and a treasure trove for finding possible elements for ongoing life," as Jane Guyer argues, "and may be the ground on which narrative and elemental assemblage become quite different, or perhaps complementary or coexisting in composing approaches to an emergent, but unknown, future, in specific times and places" (Guyer 2017:92).

Halfway through the film, both Yasmine and Jumana go through experiences that have a direct and violent impact on their bodies. One day while Yasmine is getting ready for work, her brother suddenly erupts, proclaiming that he has become the man of the house and that he will not let her go to work wearing this particular outfit (a cotton t-shirt and tight jeans). And while the mother smokes her cigarettes hiding in the bathroom, Yasmine keeps her cigarette pack in her bag and is not ashamed of smoking in public. Her brother snatches her bag and threatens to lock her in if she does not obey him and change her outfit. After an aggressive and tense argument, Yasmine leaves the house without the bag. In most of Khan's films we see that the subjects tend to end up sitting around on the stairs, waiting for things to unfold. What will happen as a result of the act of waiting in the liminal position of the stairs is unknown and always open, but something always takes flight from that point. "That point" is the limit, the point at which "we refuse to continue on this way" (McGranahan 2016:320). As Yasmine sits on the stairs, her young sister, on her way to school, brings Yasmine's bag along and gives it to her. She sits tenderly next to Yasmine and kisses her on the cheek. Yasmine goes to work, and sleeps over at the salon that night. Jumana gets concerned when she doesn't find Yasmine in the metro as she usually does. She calls her repeatedly and they eventually meet in their usual spot, a small café downtown. In this encounter, Yasmine narrates the seemingly traumatizing morning experience with her brother to Jumana, but in an affective, highly intense, deeply personal, and emotionally charged language. After describing the details of the incident, Yasmine recounts,

You know, when Yasser [her younger brother] *snatched my bag and turned it upside down and everything fell on the table, I felt I was naked. I felt that what he's telling me is that I have no rights whatsoever . . . that nothing is mine to claim . . . do you understand?*

At this point the situation itself had already passed, and Yasmine's brother had already made peace with her and apologized. However, the short yet revealing conversation between the two friends unearthed the thing that hit Yasmine most powerfully at her core. With her closest friend, Yasmine opened up about how she had made sense of that incident, how it affected and offended her. Behind this explanation lies a wish to be understood, acknowledged, contained, and perhaps repaired.

A few days later Jumana faces an even more brutal incident in the lingerie shop where she works. Her boss catches her stealing a bra that she liked but most probably could not afford. The boss sees her but does not confront her immediately. Instead, she waits until the work day is over; then, as Jumana is getting ready to leave, she yells at her to get into the fitting room and take off all her clothes, so that she can make sure Jumana has not stolen anything else. Jumana bursts into tears and swears that she hasn't stolen anything else, but the boss insists. Jumana has to go into the fitting room, leaving the door open, and strip all her clothes off to show the lady that nothing else has been stolen. She breaks down in tears in the fitting room, naked, as the boss fires her, yelling at her in humiliating language, asking her never to set foot in the shop again.

Whether and how the two friends help each other out of these stories is the question that unfolds throughout the film, always in unpredictable ways and always with a hint of uncertainty and risk. The friends' narrations of their experiences of nakedness and deep sense of vulnerability to the friend have their own language of common entanglement and construct a particular register of the world, one that I argue is different from other languages, whether personal or political. This language contains elements of genuine honesty and openness, but also guilt, confusion, and a sense of doubt about what and who one really is and how to best narrate oneself in the world. Experiences of vulnerability are undergone differently by the two friends and produce different feelings, and fears of weakness and failure to become "good" and "real" persons. The sharing of narratives continues, until the two friends stand, literally, in front of each other and mirror each other's flaws and failings.

Near the end of the film comes a moment in which the friend-ship between Jumana and Yasmine is put to the test. Early in the film, Yasmine makes up a fake story about her and Jumana's identities, occu-pations, and life conditions to two young men they had met in the metro, in an attempt to impress them. The fake story eventually gets out of their control, and although Yasmine and Jumana originally meant no harm, either to themselves or to anyone else, they end up getting caught in a trap where one of them has to uncover the truth to the men by revealing the other's truth. Yasmine had told the men that she has a beautiful voice, and that she is a member of a women's band. She arranges with an actual member of the band to pretend she is part of it, but her microphone would be turned off. She invites the man on whom she is playing the trick, who brings his friend, who brings Jumana. The three of them watch as Jasmine starts singing confidently with the other women, thinking that her microphone is not on, but it is. The song starts to fade and Yasmine continues singing, not knowing that her voice, which is actually not good at all, is being heard by everyone. The young men start laughing hysterically. After some hesitation, Jumana laughs at her as well, then stops and looks guiltily at Yasmine as she starts crying when she finds out that her lie has been been uncovered.

This scene is followed by the most intense encounter of the film. The conflict between Jumana and Yasmine leads to a fierce unravel-ing of certain truths about each friend, not only as a friend, but as a person. The setting is the metro station late at night, almost completely empty, with the two of them facing each other, not side by side as usual. The dispute starts with blame: Yasmine wonders how her friend could laugh at her truth like the strangers, and why she could not save her from embarrassment by pointing out to her that the microphone was working. How could she let the world see Yasmine's truth, which they had deliberately hidden together? How could she, even momentarily, be a part of the world's cruelty, humiliation, shaming? Jumana defends herself by saying that she had no other choice, that she did not sign up for the lie from the start, and that Yasmine should take responsibility for the consequences of her choices. They start to accuse each other of not having been a good friend after all, in the process illuminating dark

aspects of each other's personalities as individuals. They know each other's imperfections and vulnerabilities so well that they can shock each
other only by revealing each other's true selves, in an act of mirroring.
Thus friends can destroy the masks and shields that they construct in
order to live their lives among others. This moment of rupture forces
revelations. A crack of this kind that occurs in a friendship always holds
the potential for either the emergence of a more powerful bond, or a
complete break, at least until the people themselves decide, perhaps at a
later point in life, to give birth to another point of contact.

> *You are the one who decides when to lie and when to confess, you are
> the one who gets to make all the decisions? What am I, then? The
> "friend" of the heroine? The sidekick who follows you like a shadow?*
> (Khan 2005)

For the first time in the film, the camera switches angles repeatedly,
filming the confrontation from the side of each of the friends as she
speaks. They now face each other with explicit questions about how they
see each other and whether their "truths," which have always existed,
will become a barrier to the continuity of their friendship. For the first
time, Jumana and Yasmine stand on opposite platforms, not looking at
each other, not smiling at each other and joking, for each has drowned
in the weight of what has just been unveiled. The crack has happened,
and whether their friendship will endure is an open question. If it does

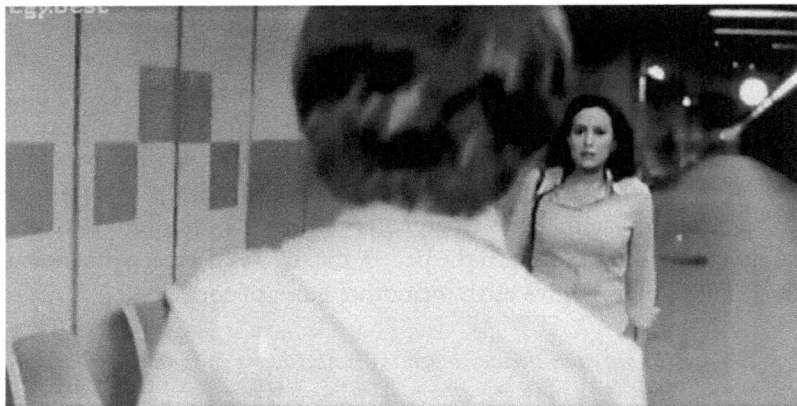

endure, the consequences are always up to the friends themselves, depending on what they can bear to know, and bear to live with, about both themselves and each other.

"Are you pure air and solitude and bread and medicine to your friend?" (Nietzsche 1972:41).
After an agonizing and sleepless night for both of the girls, they bump into each other the next day, as usual, in the metro. One is already inside the car when the other gets on. They exchange looks that are at first charged with multiple interpretations. They convey blame and uncertainty, but their continued eye contact mostly implies a mutual desire for reconnection. They keep exchanging looks that, over the

course of a few seconds, become tender and friendly. They begin smiling at each other, and eventually they begin to laugh, together and to each other but at a distance. Finally they stand up and hug. Yet this reunion is not to be understood as initiating a blank new page. If friends decide to start over, they do so from where they broke. There is no way of unknowing what friends know and learn about each other. In the case of Jumana and Yasmine, the film displays their clash in such detail that, as the audience, we sense the edge of the abyss just as acutely as they did. The reuniting of friends is always charged with the causes of the conflict or the temporary separation. The reacceptance as friends must be mutual, and it must be a process of making peace with the truths that have been uncovered about oneself in the eyes of the friend, the truths realized about the friendship, and the truths that lie in the heart of the friend, no matter how unacceptable they might have initially seemed. This narrative become clear to us as audience, however briefly, in the film's ending. The film ends with a voice-over narration by Yasmine, who once voiced her insecurity about being the heroine's sidekick, now moving beyond this tension toward a bigger question. "*Hanefdal sohab?*" (Are we going to stay friends?) Yasmine and Jumana ask each other as Jumana stands in her wedding gown, about to marry the man of her dreams. They both say " '*Alatul*" (forever) and kiss each other tenderly on the cheek.

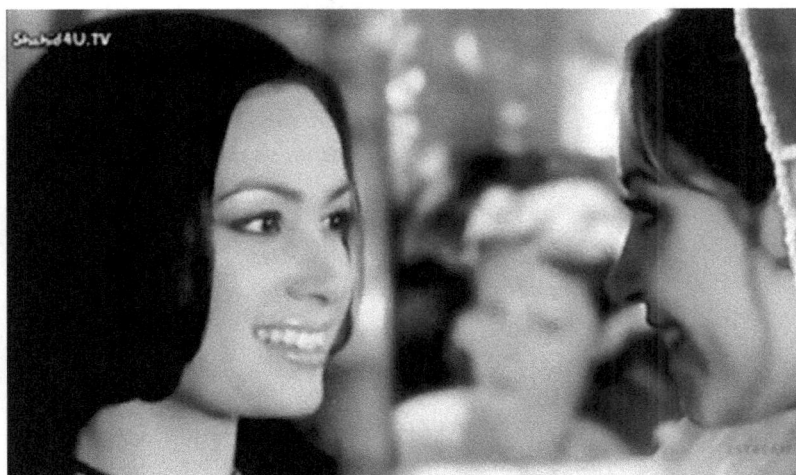

Yasmine narrated the beginning of the film; Jumana now narrates the ending. A few years later, Jumana has become a flight attendant. We see her on the phone arranging to meet with someone in the metro, and then we see Yasmine, now the mother of a child who runs to Jumana and sits on her lap as the metro starts to move. Yasmine stares out of the window and says "You know what . . . I miss Downtown." "Downtown" here stands not only for the physicality of the neighborhood and the space where their friendship was born and practiced and also almost died, but also the period in their lives in which all of this happened. Their friendship lasted and managed to survive "downtown," and the only person who can know and understand exactly what this longing is for, and what it carries, is the friend with whom she lived the experience. "Downtown" here is a place that stands for something bigger than itself. It represents not only the streets that they walked together and shared, but also a time in which they were younger, full of desire and hunger for life.

Friendship Makes and Friendship Breaks: Archives of Flesh and Blood

Half my friends are dead.
I will make you new ones, said earth.
No, give me them back, as they were, instead,
with faults and all, I cried.

Tonight I can snatch their talk
from the faint surf's drone
through the canes, but I cannot walk

on the moonlit leaves of ocean
down that white road alone,
or float with the dreaming motion

of owls leaving earth's load.
O earth, the number of friends you keep
exceeds those left to be loved.

The sea canes by the cliff flash green and silver;
they were the seraph lances of my faith,
but out of what is lost grows something stronger

that has the rational radiance of stone,
enduring moonlight, further than despair,
strong as the wind, that through dividing canes

brings those we love before us, as they were,
with faults and all, not nobler, just there. (Walcott 1993:78)

Friendship can be described as a mode of practicing the ordinary, everyday, big and small ethics of recreating a livable life, for oneself as well as for others. It is a value, a vocation, and a practice that is as much about surprise and the emergence of flows and attachments as it is about repetition and working with what is there. It is about "recognizing," "seeing," and if possible "containing" the other, as they are, without being overwhelmed by friction, or intoxicated or destroyed by the uncertainty and fluidity of the relation. At the end of the day, friendship can and does fail at many instances and for many people. Yet the kind of relatedness that I have explored here is neither pure utopia nor pure violence, and is hardly ever a project thought of as forever. The fluidity inherent in the relationship of friendship is crucial to the making and maintaining of the bond, and more importantly, for the re-creation of the friends themselves as they grow and change. Returning to the finale of *Downtown Girls*, the question "*Hanefdal sohab?*" is more like an epiphany, a question that contains its own answer, and yet also holds the space for many potential unfoldings. It places an open bet on the future. Like all true friendships it remains an encounter open to possibilities of life and death. This openness, I argue, is fundamental to friendship, and I believe it is important to theorize it as one of the main radical potentialities friendship can offer. I believe that the "crack," the encounter of critical confrontation between friends, is generative because it is a threshold where the past, that led up to the encounter, and the future, or the possible consequences of the encounter, are carefully weighed by the friends in order for a reconfiguration of some sort to take place.

In their interesting analysis, Bergman and Montgomery (2017) draw on an extensive range of sources, from Hobbes to Nietzsche to The Invisible Community, to emphasize the radical freedom offered by friendship seen as an open-ended becoming. They begin by tracing the linguistic root of the word "friend," which shares the same Indo-European root as "freedom": *fri*, or *pri*, meaning "love." Expanding on this argument, which has also been discussed by The Invisible Community, the authors ground their understanding in affect theory as it allows and enacts an attunement to the shifting capacities and openness of bodies and situations. Affect theory thus becomes a more suitable lens through which to examine an active and fluid relation like friendship—one that is always "in the middle." Overall, Bergman and Montgomery advance an argument about the generativity of the elusiveness of friendship, and the freedom that friendship entails and enacts. On the one hand, they discuss the capacity of friendship to empower people to be comfortable with who they are, which might undo the ways in which they initially internalized notions of shame, doubt, and insecurity and the "depleting patterns ingrained by capitalism and other forces of oppression" (Bergman and Montgomery 2017:6). On the other hand, they maintain that there is always a possibility that intimacy and closeness will backfire and act as sources of oppression, coercion, and manipulation. They leave us on a brief note on "difference," which can sometimes have a positive transformative effect as a starting point for the "growth of something new." However, I believe they fail to give sufficient consideration to the real-life ambiguity of personal relationships and whether all that is lacking in them is the "freedom" to make or break the toxic patterns. On the last page of their article they write: "To turn friendship into a solution or a goal is to erase the form of freedom we are getting at, which is an open-ended capacity to transform relationships" (9). However, isn't this a utopian statement in itself? Don't we in one way or another also seek a solution in and through our friendships? Don't we somehow end up needing, wishing for, and relying on the friendships in our lives to represent solidity and permanence, at least to the extent that we have invested in the friendship? My concern is that the tight coupling of the notions of freedom and openness to change with friendship might at some point lead to an overburdening of friendship as a relationship with no rules or obligations, and thus undermine the role that commitment plays in keeping friendships alive. Like any other social relationship, friendship does require a serious amount of effort in order for it to live on. I would extend the argument made by Bergman and Montgomery about the interconnection between friendship and resistance, by adding that sometimes friendship turns bitter or toxic, but to be free does not necessarily entail a clear identification of toxicity. Sometimes friendship goes on and endures, not because it empowers and supports, but despite the fact that it does not. In the next section I will elaborate on this view by briefly analyzing a recent Egyptian television series that has been highly praised by viewers and critics for the fresh, timely, and true-to-life characters and relationships it brilliantly portrayed.

To Be Answerable, One Has to Be Able to Answer

Hatha al-Masaa (This Night) (2017) represented a leap in the Egyptian drama scene, not because of the originality of the plot, but because of the authenticity of the characters and the honest depiction of their chaotic and often contradictory behaviors, sentiments, and life choices. The crafting of the characters took seriously the nuisances that cast gloom over almost all sorts of social relationships: a married couple, family members, or friends. The series script is the product of a writing workshop that included five persons, and in my opinion the collective effort immensely enhanced the richness of the final artistic production: the 30 episodes of 45 minutes each that were broadcast on Egyptian television during the month of Ramadan 2017. The series incited a boom on social media among viewers and was one of the most watched and most highly ranked among the many television works produced for Ramadan that year.

Two of the main characters of the series are two young men who, we learn, have grown up together as best friends. However, they are two very different characters. As the audience we can see that they have a rather complex history, but we do not have much access to it, as we enter the story in the middle. The series deserves a long analysis which should be the subject of a separate essay, but within the space of this chapter I wish to convey how the series managed to present a different image of friendship, in the sense that it is thicker and bolder than the usual representations of friendship on the Egyptian television screen. Samir is kind, polite, responsible, well educated, well dressed, reserved, and very

diligent in his job as a private driver for a businessman. Sony works in a
mobile-phone shop, is a hacker who spies on people's personal phones
for fun and sometimes exploits them as a result, a womanizer, a trouble-
maker, witty, the confusing kind of on-screen villain. But the brilliance
of the series lies exactly in the fact that he is not a typical villain. He is
a person with flaws, who causes much damage to himself and to those
around him, including his best friend Samir, yet he constantly eludes
the category of the "bad" person or the "bad" friend. Perhaps because the
character is very smart, he confuses everyone by not allowing himself to
be simply and bluntly categorized as one thing or the other. Sony loves
Samir, but we understand that although they share a history of unethi-
cal digital spying on women's lives using their social media profiles, they
do not share a corresponding present. Samir abandoned digital hacking
and cyberbullying after he exposed the secret life of the wife of one of
his friends and caused her murder. Samir then pursued other goals in
life, such as a more stable career, while Sony continued his cyberspying.
Samir developed a potential romance with a young woman, while Sony
only attracted women by threating to disclose their personal pictures
publicly on the Internet. It becomes obvious at some point in the series
that the choices each friend made individually have affected not only
the life of that person, but also his friendship with the other.

When the drama escalates to an intense conflict between the two
friends, it is a malicious confrontation that erupts like a volcano. Like
Jumana and Yasmine, the two friends confront each other both physi-
cally and metaphorically. The encounter takes place in an old and empty
film theatre, their secret spot and their usual hangout. In a sense it
resembles the "downtown" of Juamana and Yasmine. They face each
other in the aisle between the seats, while Samir's younger brother, who
is also an essential part of the group, stands between them trying to
defuse the situation. Again, in this moment of confrontation between
close friends, they bring out and face each other's truths and their own,
which are dangerous and painful. Samir begins the fight by blaming
Sony for all the trouble he has been causing for everyone, including a
young woman they both happen to like. Sony does not try to exonerate
himself, but reminds Samir that he used to be like him too, and that as
a matter of fact he caused much worse trouble. He also says that their
brother-like friendship has been no peaceful or innocent journey. In

his own defense, Sony tells Samir that he is just like him, if not worse, but that the problem is that he does not wish to be true to himself or honest with other people about who he truly is. As the audience we know for a fact that Samir changed, and did his best to become a better person. Perhaps he would like to reverse his past, erasing the previous versions of himself that are causing him shame and guilt. Yet friendship is "an archive of flesh and blood" (as my friend Haytham al-Wardany once wrote to me), whereby the history of "us" as individuals as well as friends, over different periods of time, is preserved quite differently than it is in any other relationship.

To be more specific, the renderings of our lives as they exist within our old, close friends constitute archives of experiences, both large and small, inscribed in informal languages and codes of intimacy between friends. Those unofficial, thrown-together archives of being and becoming eventually form valuable reservoirs that hold what the friends as persons once were, what they currently are, and a sense of what they might become. The good friend is perhaps not free of judgment, but is certainly the one who "remembers," the one whom I can count on to recall, recite, and renarrate my life for me—sometimes with accuracy, other times with bias, at times illuminating certain aspects while shadowing others. This archive does not aim at accreditation or validation of any kind. It is tremendously interesting to think about the moments in which there comes an urge to bring to light parts of it for purposes of defending an image of oneself or an image of the friendship itself.

> *A friendship is not based on the happenstance of sharing and passion, one that seems no more than a stroke of good luck. Rather, it also involves what we might call a tending to, in the sense that one tends to one's garden. . . . This tending to a relationship involves a recognition of the role of the past, of the personal history of friends.* (May 2012:74)

I argue that sustaining this entanglement constitutes, in many ways, a history of friends' own making. I have argued throughout the chapter, by following Jumana, Yasmine, Samir, and Sony, that for friends, the continuity or the flow of the relationship depends mainly on the extent to which friends are able to not merely return to a singular truth or essence that had brought them together, but rather to engender new territories of connectedness and realms of relatedness and empathy. I propose that friendship thus enables a space of dwelling in the sense that the friend continuously performs, if allowed, an act of "witnessing" to the life of the other. "Giving and receiving, wherein lives are rendered answerable to one another, is the very impulse that keeps it flowing" (Ingold 2017b:2). The acts of witnessing, sharing, and leaning on each other in different circumstances results in the creation of a knot, in which the strands are interlaced and tightened. "In a world where things are continually coming into being through processes of growth and movement—that is, in a world of life—knotting is the fundamental principle of coherence" (Ingold 2016:2). According to Ingold, the necessity and vitality of the knot lies in active attentiveness and commitment to the movement of things and to the ways the friends want to go; it admits of movement "as both its condition and its consequence" (Ingold 2017b:3). Attention, for Ingold, is a practice of care that lies in its resonance with the movements of the things to which it attends, in its "going along WITH them" (Ingold 2017b:3). To care for people we need to make ourselves present to them as the particular persons we are, but we must also allow them into our presence so that they can speak. Ingold offers an understanding that goes beyond giving explanations or justifications for one's becomings; he suggests a notion of care that entails listening to what others have to tell us, which also demands that we respond in kind. "It is, as Mauss taught us, a matter of discharging an ontological debt, of giving back to the world and its inhabitants what we owe them for their own formation" (Ingold 2017b:13).

Inspired by the fictional friendships explored in this chapter, I have sought to show that the meanings attached to notions of vulnerability and nakedness, as well as notions about the layered truths of us as individuals, begin to move in new routes if seen from the vantage point of friendship. The ways in which our close friends know us are significant and varied, and certainly vaster and more complicated than is usually thought and said. The kind of friendship that involves an accumulation of experiences resembles an "archive," not of any official and impersonal nature, but as Haytham writes, "an archive of flesh and blood."[8] The word "archive" here denotes a historical yet ongoing account or record of the friends' lives. This archive as a project runs against the hegemonic definition of archiving as an act of documenting and preserving a "past," because this idea of friendship as an archive must necessarily be an active acknowledgment of the friend as an ever-changing human being in an open-ended becoming. I have also argued that one must retain a critical stance toward the claims of the open-ended flows and becomings of friendship, so as not to romanticize or over-determine the freedom needed for or achieved by means of friendship.

---

8   Email from Berlin, 29 October 2017.

CHAPTER 5

Mafish Sahib Yetsahib . . .
O My Friends, There Is No Friend:
An Ode to Friendship, an Ode to the Loss of It

Vignette: O My Friends, There Is No Friend

I read and re-read Derrida's Politics of Friendship, *and I still struggled with it. My reading list was crowded and the book remained a riddle, a mystery that I was unable to decipher no matter how many times I tried to read it. One thing that came to my mind is that if I could share it with a friend or a group of friends (who knows, perhaps Derrida intended the book to be read in this way), through collaboration and group discussion the book might become easier to grasp. I asked Rashid, the one passionate philosophy geek in my life, if he had read it and he said he had not, but he showed much interest and genuine enthusiasm to read it and help me understand it. He started reading it and he created a shareable online document where he could upload notes to share with me, and quotes, excerpts from the book, that he thought I should focus on. Not long afterward, we were on the phone when Rashid threw in what seemed like a random thought: "Have you ever noticed that Derrida's first sentence ('O my friend, there is no friend') is the same thing as 'Mafish sahib yetsaheb'?" "True! It is really that, it is really the very same sentence! Oh my god, bravo! How come no one ever noticed that before now?" We both burst into laughter. It made so much sense to me. Perfect sense, in fact.*

"Mafish sahib yetsahib" (There is no friend to befriend) is an Egyptian *mahraganat*[9] song that came out in 2015, performed by Shobbeik Lobbeik. Shobbeik Lobbeik is a band of three Alexandrian young men—Hassan Elbrens, Nasser Ghandi, and Fares Hemeida—who come from a lower-middle-class neighborhood in Montazah, Alexandria called Ezbet Mohsen. Hassan Elbrens originally wrote the song, to be performed at a family wedding. From there it expanded far beyond what the band members had initially imagined. The song achieved an immediate success upon its release and became a viral phenomenon, picking up over 20 million views on YouTube within the first 60 days of its release. Three years later, it was still one of the most popular tunes played in shops, street cafés (*ahwa*s), weddings, and microbuses. Even television commercials still rework the familiar tune of the song, changing the lyrics to whatever serves the commercial content of the ad.

Every time I stumble upon the song, or deliberately play it, I cannot help but think about the moment that a possible "imaginary" relation was formed when my friend juxtaposed the Egyptian "There is no friend to befriend" against Jacques Derrida's "O my friends, there is no friend," which is itself a quotation of a quotation. Derrida is quoting from Montaigne a phrase that Montaigne in turn attributes to Aristotle: "*o philoi, oudeis philos*," which "Aristotle was used to repeating" (Derrida 1988:632). The suggestive connection, the astonishing resonance, the interactive co-constitution of relation that occurred between my friend and me, reading, thinking, and talking together, opened up a radical potentiality to me. The potential lies precisely in the ways in which our corresponding thought processes activated a particular (and playful) power inherent in the sphere of openness (and intimacy) offered by the relationship of friendship. What this incident has possibly opened up for me, other than the sheer delight and joy of the encounter, is a question on the co-constitution as well as the passing-on of knowledge(s) between friends. In this light, friendship can be seen as an integral component of the "experiment" and "experience" of being in the world as an open sphere that makes possible the "co-presence of potentials"

---

9   *Mahraganat*, also known as street or *sha'bi* music, is a genre of Egyptian dance music created by working-class Egyptian youth around the fall of Mubarak's regime. It is characterized by its high-energy pulsing beats, its bold and unrestrained lyrics, and its contentious messages.

(Massumi 2015:5). Following this argument that friendship is precisely this "active open-endedness," I also argue that the opposite completely obliterates the possibility of friendship. That is, the moment that friendship constricts the fluidity of the processes of becoming, it annihilates the condition of its possibility and inevitably ends up dissolving.

Friendship: A Suspension Between the No Longer and the Not Yet

The continuity of life—and hence of knowledge—requires of every being that it should play its part in bringing other lives into being and sustaining them for however long it takes for the latter, in turn, to engender further life. It follows that all life, and all knowing, is intrinsically social. Life is one long conversation. More precisely, it is a tangled web of concurrent conversations, all going on at once, that weave into and around one another. They flow, spinning here and there into topics like eddies in a stream. And they have three distinguishing properties. First, conversations are processes: they carry on. Secondly, conversations are open-ended: they do not aim towards a fixed destination or a final conclusion, for everything that might be said invites a follow-on. Thirdly, conversations are dialogical. They are not solitary but go on between and among people. It is from these dialogical engagements that knowledge continually emerges. To join a conversation is to be ever-present at the cusp where ideas are on the point of making their appearance, of taking shape. (Ingold 2017a:97)

The interlacing or joining of lives, like that of strands forming a knot, always comes into being in the middle of lives, along processes of growth and movement. In his article "On Human Correspondence" (2017b) the anthropologist Tim Ingold advances an extremely generative argument on the social lives of human beings. Correspondence, as Ingold proposes, is the entwining and joining of lives along lines and processes of growth and movement, acts of giving and receiving, and forces of tension and friction that are always in continual transformation. The interpenetration of lives in the mesh of the social world resembles knotting, the process by which two strands of string or yarn are interlaced and pulled tight, forming a coherent knot. The stickiness of the knot, which is a metaphor for the tightness of the human bond, is by no means predetermined, but is constantly born out of practices of care and continuous attention that move in resonance with the movements of the things to which it attends. To Ingold, attention (which he prefers to call "attention-ality") is "longitudinal"; in other words, it is an attunement to trajectories as they unfold that extends along their pathways of becoming. It is an awareness *with* before it is ever awareness *of*. I have given the example of "witnessing" as an act of attention that is sensitive to and mindful of the movement of things (chapter 2). Ingold proposes a way of thinking about attentiveness that allows different paces: "We can recognize a movement, and respond to it, before we ever fix it in our sights" (2017b:12). As such, this mode of care and attentiveness must always be understood as a form of movement, a leaping ahead that concerns not only being but also the possibility of becoming something else. As such, Ingold's knot, "where lives are rendered answerable to one another" (Ingold 2017b:2), provides a way to imagine social life in its ongoingness and its continual differentiation.

Let us begin with: how am I to listen to you? (Irigaray 1996:115)

It is the summer of 2016 and I am in the middle of the beginning of what could be called a research frenzy. My eyes gleam every time I stumble upon a new text on friendship. Between the library and the internet, I first slowly and steadily familiarize myself with the foundational texts and philosophies on friendship written by the canonical figures of radical thought, and second, I collect and study every other textual, visual, and audible material I come across through my own research or by asking friends. It started to pop up in our conversations, first as the simple question of "Is there a favorite book, a film, a poem, or a song that strikes you as related to friendship that you like? Something that either has friendship as its main theme or that alludes to it, literally or metaphorically? Or whose protagonists are maybe best friends?"

One friend (Alaa) immediately mentioned Sufi poetry, pieces by Hafiz and Rumi that she described as the most enchanting, even entrancing, on the love, goodness, purity, and kindness between friends. She also advised me to look into the genealogy of the Arabic words for "friend." For example: the friend with whom you chat at night has a name, *samir*; the friend who accompanies you in travel has a name, *rafiq* (which is also used historically in the context of political comrades); the close friend has a name, *sahib*. We tried to identify the meanings attached to each, and to determine whether or not these terms are still being used in the sense of "friend" in contemporary Egyptian or the broader Middle Eastern culture.

Another friend (Mourad) associated the theme of friendship with films, most of which belonged to Mohammed Khan's cinematic oeuvre. Mourad is a scriptwriter, and for many years he worked as a writer in the "Culture" section of a well-known Egyptian newspaper. There he published numerous film reviews, some of them dealing with the philosophy of film. He was the one who reintroduced me to the filmography of Mohammed Khan and the importance of the theme of friendship in his works, how central it is to the lives of his protagonists and integral to the plot of his films.

A third friend (Nihal) spoke of the January 25th revolution, particularly the "Battle of the Camel" (2 February 2011). She recounted a near-death experience near Tahrir Square, in which a man attacked her with a sword, placed it on her neck, and almost, almost killed her but didn't.

I was in the middle of Talaat Harb Street not knowing where to go. I had just taken my son out of the square and made sure he was safely out of the area of Downtown. I was trying to return to Tahrir Square when this man attacked me. He ran toward me, with a sword, and some friends were behind me and saw the encounter. He just placed it on my neck; he neither said anything nor stuck it in my throat. Luckily a few of my friends were behind me, in the same area, and they rescued me. They also decided that I should not return to the square, and they took me to a place, the last safe haven that wasn't yet burned with the flying Molotovs that were everywhere by then in Downtown. This place had been the premises of some political party, but now it was a site where some of the wounded and the scattered activists had started to gather and take shelter, friends as well as strangers. The reason why I am recounting this incident is what happened at the next moment. There was a young lady with us in the same place, whom I had known from before. In the midst of all this she looked at all of us, everyone gathered under this roof, and said, "You know, if we make it out of here alive, we will never forget each other." I don't really have any feelings for the sword incident, except that it was traumatic. But this, what the girl said, is what still makes my eyes tear up every time I remember. What I am saying is that I was not really aware that we were living something "big" and "historic," because when she first said that I remember feeling like "What does she mean and why is she saying this?" But now it makes a lot of sense.

I immediately asked Nihal, with piercing curiosity, "And do you remember everyone who was there?"

She answered: "Every single person."

My chat with Nihal was exceptionally difficult to decipher. It took me some time to understand why exactly this story was the first thing that suggested itself to her when I asked her about friendship. On the one hand, I fully realize that the constellation of fragments, memories, stories, and references that my friends shared with me are not to be understood as eternal inscriptions of what friendship should mean to everyone, or even to them. On the other hand, it was important to think through those chosen items in their full particularity for the value they carry, because, after all, there is no definitive and all-encompassing narrative of friendship, or of what it means to different people and how they envision it.

Why do we acknowledge only our textual sources but not the ground we walk, the ever-changing skies, mountains and rivers, rocks and trees, the houses we inhabit and the tools we use, not to mention the innumerable companions, both non-human animals and fellow humans, with which and with whom we share our lives? They are constantly inspiring us, challenging us, telling us things. If our aim is to read the world, as I believe it ought to be, then the purpose of written texts should be to enrich our reading so that we might be better advised by, and responsive to, what the world is telling us. (Ingold 2011:xii)

Sharing experiences, memories, sentiments, secrets, ideas, dreams, desires, fears, tragedies, large and small everyday nuances between friends involves a creation and an assertion of power, not over others or over events, but rather a power that is an extended capacity to work and think through things together differently. We are hence enabled, as Michael Jackson states, "to grasp experiences that confound us, react to events that overwhelm us, and become creators rather than mere creatures of circumstance" (2012:48). This sharing may not always happen in the form of "storytelling" that Jackson refers to, yet it resembles storytelling in the ways in which it engenders an endless capacity for creativity and inventiveness, combining acts of remembering and acts of imagination, that allows the emergence of new revelations and relations, through interactive mediation with the friend.

"But the Knot Remembers Everything": On Growing Out of Friendship

> *"I might never meet you again, Nigel, but there's still the chance that I will. It's like we talk of infinity: two parallel lines meet at infinity, and the rest; but we don't really understand infinity at all. . . . Well, I've bared my soul to you tonight, Nigel. Bared my soul."* (Bell and Coleman 1999:114)

Going back to Ingold's "knot" as the binding of lifelines in a meshwork of entangled relations, which I find to be an incredibly useful, productive, and inspiring metaphor, I would like to imagine and examine the end of friendships as a phenomenon much like the untying of knots. Ingold describes the untying situation not as an event of "disarticulation" or "decomposition": "It is rather a casting off, whence lines once bound together go their separate ways" (Ingold 2017b:5). As I was listening again to the many recorded notes, interviews, and chats from my fieldwork period and going through my written field notes, I was stunned by the intensity of the encounters, the intimacy that felt so unbearably real. While some of the lines of life continued, others did not.

This research mainly started as a daydream in an apartment occupied by two Alexandrian friends in Downtown Cairo in the summer of 2017. I was fortunate to have access to the lives of the two young men, their shared domestic life, their friendship. There was something particularly fascinating about them, coming from the same hometown yet living and working here in Cairo, perhaps because this act of independence and relocation is something that I have not experienced myself (but always dreamed of), or because the movement from the city of Alexandria to the capital has always been an intriguing phenomenon to me. I remember that the physical manifestation of movement was tremendously overt in that apartment. The apartment spoke of "home" and "stillness" but simultaneously screamed "movement" and "drifting," as if the life that took place therein were always suspended on the verge between both. The backpacks and suitcases were hardly ever either fully loaded or fully emptied. Something was always ready to be installed in Cairo, while something else was always ready to go back to Alexandria, unfinished. This place and those two friends inspired a large part of this research, and my gratitude to them is infinite. However, while this manuscript is a text that will live on, this context that I have been trying to describe had already died. We are no longer linked as we were a couple of years ago and this home is now alien to me. "Home is where I take up such a tiny portion of the memory foam; home is a splintered word," writes Karen Green (2013). I move back to this apartment only inside my head now through the elusive and fragmented memory of a distant friendship, and put together its bits and pieces like a jigsaw to create meaning.

Friendship is not possible without the correspondence of its constituents, with the friends answering and responding to each other's lives. Every relation, like every process, every encounter, every life, is itself a mode of becoming that has its own force, pace, and time. We constantly become 'more' and 'other' than our own histories through our engagement with the dynamic environments of humans, animals, materialities, objects. Becomings are the various "processes of the production of things, processes that transform states of matter, processes that enable and complicate life" (Grosz 2011:13). It is the entwining and interweaving of lives and of these ever-extending trajectories in becoming that comprise the texture of friendship and of life. I argue that friendship is, before all else, about becoming. It sometimes seems to me that friendship can only be understood in the complex and open-ended paradox of becoming, as something that is constantly moved toward but never really reached, never fully fathomed, never fully realized. It can best be described as a movement along paths rather than a being-anchored in spaces of safety, ideas, ideologies, or particular ambitions about "how things should be." As Biehl and Locke put it so beautifully, "Distinct from potentiality and not reducible to causality or outcomes, *becoming* is characterized by the indeterminacies that keep history open" (2017:6). Being friends is not the same as becoming friends. I would say that the former is not imaginable without constant attempts at the latter.

It is worth considering whether Ingold's metaphor of the untying of the knot as a simple "casting off" that "does not break things into pieces" remains valid when applied to human relationships—although later in the same article he does treat "loss" and "grief" upon the parting of lives, yet very briefly. Perhaps there is something to be learned from Hassan Elbrens; there is no friend out there to *befriend*. Perhaps one can at best seek to become friends, time and again, with those who extend their hands to shake ours, who open their eyes to witness what we see, who lend their ears in an effort to listen to what we have to say, and who split their hearts open to be able to understand that which remains unsaid, that which lingers in its solitude, dangerous and untouched.

During the months it took me to write this manuscript, since writing is mostly a solitary activity, I largely stayed away from my own friends, but they did not stay away from me. In my defense I say: I am writing about friendship . . . I am writing about you! and soon after, words fail me. This piece of writing is at best an ode to friendship and at worst a flawed entrance onto perplexing, complicated, and risky grounds. What I hope I managed to safely maintain, both at heart and in writing, are the precious voices of my friends, without suffocating them or assimilating them into mine. The source of the strength of friendship and its main domain, my friend Haytham believes, is in the "trembling vibrations of the friend's voice." For him, everything else, like facial features, can be said to belong to the other loves, the family, the state, or one's age. You can age, move to another country, get married, get a job, lose a job, but your voice remains with me, remains as familiar to me as it has always been; it belongs to me and to our friendship.

No society, then, but worlds. And no war against society either: to wage war against a fiction is to give it substance. There's no social sky above our heads, there's us and the ensemble of ties, friendships, enmities, and actual proximities and distances that we experience.

There are only sets of us, eminently situated powers, and their ability to ramify throughout the endlessly decomposing and recomposing social carcass. A swarming of worlds, a world made up of a whole slew of worlds, and traversed therefore by conflicts between them, by attractions and repulsions. To construct a world is to create an order, make a place or not for each thing, each being, each proclivity, and give thought to that place, change it if need be. . . . It's not a question of choosing between the care we devote to what we are constructing and our political striking force. Our striking force is composed of the very intensity of what we are living, of the joy emanating from it, of the forms of expression invented there, of a collective ability to withstand stresses that is attested by our force. (Invisible Committee 2015)

References

Print and Online Sources

Abourahme, N. 2014. "Ruinous City, Ruinous Time: Future Suspended and the Science Fiction of the Present," *City*, 18(4–5): 577–582.

Ahmed, S. 2010. *The Promise of Happiness*. Durham, NC: Duke University Press.

———. 2014. *The Cultural Politics of Emotion*. 2nd ed. Edinburgh: Edinburgh University Press.

Arendt, H. 1998. *The Human Condition*. Chicago and London: University of Chicago Press.

Badhwar, N. K., ed. 1993. *Friendship: A Philosophical Reader*. Ithaca, NY: Cornell University Press.

Barad, K. 2012. "On Touching—The Inhuman that Therefore I Am," *Differences*, 23(3): 206–223.

Behar, R. 1996. *The Vulnerable Observer: Anthropology that Breaks Your Heart*. Boston: Beacon Press.

Bell, S., and S. Coleman, eds. 1999. *The Anthropology of Friendship*. Oxford: Berg.

Benjamin, W. 1978. *Reflections: Essays, Aphorisms, Autobiographical Writings*. Trans. E. Jephcott; ed. P. Demetz. New York: Harcourt Brace Jovanovich.

Berardi, F. 2009. *The Soul at Work: From Alienation to Autonomy*. Los Angeles: Semiotext(e).

Bergman, C., and N. Montgomery. 2017. "Friendship is a Root of Freedom." January 9. Retrieved from https://joyfulmilitancy.com/2017/12/11/friendship-as-a-root-of-freedom/

Berlant, L. 1998. "Intimacy: A Special Issue," *Critical Inquiry*, 24(2): 281–288.

———. 2008a. *The Female Complaint: The Unfinished Business of Sentimentality in American Culture*. Durham, NC: Duke University Press.

———. 2008b. "Thinking about Feeling Historical," *Emotion, Space and Society*, 1(1): 4–9.

———. 2010. "Cruel Optimism." In M. Gregg and G. J. Seigworth, eds., *The Affect Theory Reader*, 93–117. Durham, NC: Duke University Press.

———. 2011a. *Cruel Optimism*. Durham, NC: Duke University Press.

———. 2011b. "A Properly Political Concept of Love: Three Approaches in Ten Pages," *Cultural Anthropology*, 26(4): 683–691.

———. 2012a. "Cruel Optimism, Becoming Event: A Response." December 10. Retrieved from http://bcrw.barnard.edu/wp-content/uploads/2012/Public-Feelings-Responses/Lauren-Berlant-Cruel-Optimism-Becoming-Event.pdf

———. 2012b. *Desire/Love*. Brooklyn, NY: Punctum Books.

———. 2015. "A Momentary Anesthesia of the Heart," *International Journal of Politics, Culture, and Society*, 28(3): 273–281.

———. 2016. "The Commons: Infrastructures for Troubling Times," *Environment and Planning D: Society and Space*, 34(3): 393–419.

———. N.d. "Supervalent Thought." https://supervalentthought.com/

Berlant, L., and E. McCabe. 2011. "Depressive Realism: An Interview with Lauren Berlant," *Hypocrite Reader*, 5.

Berlant, L., and J. Prosser. 2011. "Life Writing and Intimate Publics: A Conversation with Lauren Berlant," *Biography*, 34(1): 180–187.

Biehl, J. 2013. "Ethnography in the Way of Theory," *Cultural Anthropology*, 28(4): 573–597.

Biehl, J., and P. Locke, eds. 2017. *Unfinished: The Anthropology of Becoming*. Durham, NC: Duke University Press.

Blanchot, M. 1988. *The Unavowable Community*. Barrytown, NY: Station Hill.

Blanchot, M., and L. Hill. 2000. "For Friendship," *Oxford Literary Review*, 22:25–38. Retrieved from http://www.jstor.org/stable/44030957

Blanchot, M., and E. Rottenberg. 1997. *Friendship*. Trans. E. Rottenberg. Stanford, CA: Stanford University Press.

Bunnell, T., S. Yea, L. Peake, T. Skelton, and M. Smith. 2012. "Geographies of Friendships," *Progress in Human Geography*, 36(4), 490–507.

Butler, J. 2006. *Precarious Life: The Powers of Mourning and Violence.* London and New York: Verso.

———. 2009. *Frames of War: When Is Life Grievable?* London and New York: Verso.

Carsten, J., ed. 2000. *Cultures of Relatedness: New Approaches to the Study of Kinship.* Cambridge, UK: Cambridge University Press.

Coward, M. 2012. "Between Us in the City: Materiality, Subjectivity, and Community in the Era of Global Urbanization," *Environment and Planning D: Society and Space*, 30(3): 468–481.

Das, V., M. D. Jackson, A. Kleinman, and B. Singh, eds. 2014. *The Ground Between: Anthropologists Engage Philosophy.* Durham, NC: Duke University Press.

Davis, H., and P. Sarlin. 2009. "'On the Risk of a New Relationality': An Interview with Lauren Berlant and Michael Hardt," *On the Commons*, 2(3): 18.

Deleuze, G. 1995. *Negotiations, 1972–1990.* New York: Columbia University Press.

Deleuze, G., and F. Guattari. 1994. *What Is Philosophy?* New York: Columbia University Press.

———. 2004. *A Thousand Plateaus: Capitalism and Schizophrenia.* Trans. B. Massumi. London: Continuum.

———. 2006. *Two Regimes of Madness.* Ed. David Lapoujade, trans. Ames Hodges and Mike Taormina. New York: Semiotext(e).

Derrida, J. 1988. "The Politics of Friendship," *The Journal of Philosophy*, 85(11): 632–644. Retrieved from http://www.jstor.org/stable/2026938

———. 1997. *Politics of Friendship.* London and New York: Verso.

Desai, A., and E. Killick, eds. 2010. *The Ways of Friendship: Anthropological Perspectives.* New York: Berghahn Books.

Dosse, F. 2010. *Gilles Deleuze and Félix Guattari: Intersecting Lives.* New York: Columbia University Press.

Eagleton, T. 2015. "What Is Hope?" In *Hope without Optimism*, 39–89. New Haven and London: Yale University Press.

Eve, M. 2002. "Is Friendship a Sociological Topic?," *European Journal of Sociology/Archives Européennes de Sociologie*, 43(3):386–409.

Federici, S. 2008. "Precarious Labour: A Feminist Perspective." Blog post, "In the Middle of a Whirlwind." Retrieved May 2017 from https://inthemiddleofthewhirlwind.wordpress.com/precarious-labor-a-feminist-viewpoint/

Frayne, D. 2015. *The Refusal of Work: The Theory and Practice of Resistance to Work.* London: Zed Books.

Gregg, M., and G. J. Seigworth, eds. 2010. *The Affect Theory Reader.* Durham, NC: Duke University Press.

Green, K. L. 2013. *Bough Down.* Los Angeles: Siglio.

Grosz, E. 2011. *Becoming Undone: Darwinian Reflections on Life, Politics, and Art.* Durham, NC: Duke University Press.

Guyer, J. I. 2017. "Aftermaths and Recuperations in Anthropology (The 2016 Sir James George Frazer Memorial Lecture)," *HAU: Journal of Ethnographic Theory,* 7(1): 81–103.

Haddad, F. 2012. "Malhamat awal Mayo (The First of May Saga)." Vol. 2 of *Al-A'mal al-Kamela* (The Complete Works). Cairo: Egyptian General Book Organization.

Hage, G., ed. 2009. *Waiting.* Melbourne: Melbourne University Publishing.

Haraway, D. J. 2016. *Staying with the Trouble: Making Kin in the Chthulucene.* Durham, NC: Duke University Press.

Hardt, M. 1999. "Affective Labour," *Boundary 2*(26): 89–100.

Heidegger, M. 1971. "Building Dwelling Thinking," *Poetry, Language, Thought,* 154:143–159.

Herman, G. 1987. *Ritualised Friendship and the Greek City.* Cambridge, UK: Cambridge University Press.

Illich, I., and J. Brown. "We the People," KPFA Radio, Berkeley, CA, 22 March.

Ingold, T. 2011. *Being Alive: Essays on Movement, Knowledge and Description.* Milton Park, UK: Taylor & Francis.

———. 2017a. *Correspondences.* Aberdeen: University of Aberdeen.

———. 2017b. "On Human Correspondence," *Journal of the Royal Anthropological Institute,* 23(1): 9–27.

Invisible Committee. 2015. *To Our Friends.* Trans. Robert Hurley. New York: Semiotext(e).

Irigaray, L.. 1996. *I Love to You.* Trans. Alison Martin. New York: Routledge.

Irigaray, L., C. Busson, J. Mooney, H. Bostic, and S. Pluhacek. 2002. "Being Two, How Many Eyes Have We?," *Paragraph*, 25(3): 143–151. Retrieved from http://www.jstor.org/stable/43263703

Jackson, M. 2012. *Lifeworlds: Essays in Existential Anthropology.* Chicago: University of Chicago Press.

Kathiravelu, L. 2013. "Friendship and the Urban Encounter: Towards a Research Agenda." Max Planck Institute for the Study of Religious and Ethnic Diversity, Working Paper 13-10.

Kathiravelu, L., and T. Bunnell. 2018. "Introduction: Urban Friendship Networks: Affective Negotiations and Potentialities of Care," *Urban Studies*, 55(3): 491–504.

Kaufman, E. 2001. *The Delirium of Praise: Bataille, Blanchot, Deleuze, Foucault, Klossowski.* Baltimore and London: Johns Hopkins University Press.

Lambert, G. 2008. "Deleuze and the Political Ontology of 'The Friend' (Philos)." In I. Buchanan and N. Thoburn, eds., *Deleuze and Politics*, 35–53. Edinburgh: Edinburgh University Press.

Latour, B. 2005. *Reassembling the Social: An Introduction to Actor-Network Theory.* Oxford, UK: Oxford University Press.

Lewis, C. S. 1950. *The Lion, the Witch and the Wardrobe: The Chronicles of Narnia*, vol. 1. GoodBook LLC.

———. 1993. "Friendship: The Least Necessary Love." In N. K. Badhwar, ed., *Friendship: A Philosophical Reader*, 39–47. Ithaca, NY: Cornell University Press.

Lingis, A. 1994. *The Community of Those Who Have Nothing in Common.* Bloomington: Indiana University Press.

Malinowski, B. 1922. *Argonauts of the Western Pacific.* Prospect Heights, IL: Waveland Press, 1 (1954).

Massumi, B. 2015. *The Politics of Affect.* Cambridge, UK: Polity Press.

———. 2017. *The Principle of Unrest: Activist Philosophy in the Expanded Field.* London: Open Humanities Press.

May, T. 2012. *Friendship in an Age of Economics: Resisting the Forces of Neoliberalism.* Lanham, MD: Lexington Books.

McGranahan, C. 2016. "Theorizing Refusal: An Introduction," *Cultural Anthropology*, 31(3): 319–325.

Merwin, W. S. 1969. *The Moving Target: Poems.* New York: Penguin.

Nagar, R. 2014. *Muddying the Waters: Coauthoring Feminisms across Scholarship and Activism*. Urbana: University of Illinois Press.

Navaro, Yael. 2017. "Diversifying Affect," *Cultural Anthropology*, 32(2): 209–214. https://doi.org/10.14506/ca32.2.05.

Negri, A. 1999. "Value and Affect," *Boundary 2*, 26(2): 77–88.

Nietzsche, F. 1972. *Thus Spoke Zarathustra: A Book for Everyone and No One*. New York: Penguin Books.

———. 2001. "Request." In B. Williams, ed., *The Gay Science: With a Prelude in German Rhymes and an Appendix of Songs*, trans. J. Nauckhoff, 15–16. Cambridge, UK: Cambridge University Press.

Obeid, M. 2010. "Friendship, Kinship and Sociality in a Lebanese Town." In M. Obeid et al., eds., *The Ways of Friendship: Anthropological Perspectives*, 93–113. Oxford: Berghahn Books.

Pakaluk, M., ed. 1991. *Other Selves: Philosophers on Friendship*. Indianapolis: Hackett Publishing.

Pitt-Rivers, J. 1973. "The Kith and the Kin." In J. Goody, ed., *The Character of Kinship*, 89–105. Cambridge, UK: Cambridge University Press.

Rabinow, P. 1997. *Ethics, Subjectivity and Truth: The Essential Works of Foucault 1954–1984*, vol. 1. New York: New Press.

Ridge, L. 2013. "Mother." Lola Ridge—Poems. Academy of American Poets. Poets.org. https://poets.org/poem/mother-1.

Roach, T. 2012. *Friendship as a Way of Life: Foucault, AIDS, and the Politics of Shared Estrangement*. Albany: State University of New York Press.

Roy, A. 2017a. Interview by S. Ansari, July 10. Retrieved from http://www.chatelaine.com/living/books/arundhati-roy-interview/

———. 2017b. *The Ministry of Utmost Happiness*. New York: Knopf.

Sedgwick, E. K. 2003. "Paranoid Reading and Reparative Reading, or, You're So Paranoid, You Probably Think This Introduction Is about You." In E. K. Sedgwick, ed., *Touching Feeling: Affect, Pedagogy, Performativity*, 123–151. Durham: Oxford University Press.

Segall, A. 2011. "Critical Ethnography and the Invocation of Voice: From the Field/in the Field—Single Exposure, Double Standard?" *International Journal of Qualitative Studies in Education*, 14(4): 579–592.

Sepehri, S., and M. Shahegh. 1988. "Address." *Sohrab Sepehri, Neshani, Address, Where Is the Friend's House*. http://www.perlit.sailorsite.net/Mahvash/sohrab_neshani.html

Simone, A. 2004. "People as Infrastructure: Intersecting Fragments in Johannesburg," *Public Culture*, 16(3): 407–429.

———. 2016. "Passing Things Along: (In)completing Infrastructure," *New Diversities*, 17(2): 151–162.

Stavrides, S. 2007. "Heterotopias and the Experience of Porous Urban Space." In K. A. Franck, ed., *Loose Space: Possibility and Diversity in Urban Life*, 174–192. London and New York: Routledge.

Stewart, K. 2007. *Ordinary Affects*. Durham, NC: Duke University Press.

———. 2008. "Weak Theory in an Unfinished World," *Journal of Folklore Research*, 45(1): 71–82.

———. 2011. "Atmospheric Attunements," *Environment and Planning D: Society and Space*, 29(3), 445–453.

———. 2012a. "Pockets," *Communication and Critical/Cultural Studies*, 9(4): 365–368.

———. 2012b. "Precarity's Forms," *Cultural Anthropology*, 27(3): 518–525.

———. 2017. "In the World that Affect Proposed," *Cultural Anthropology*, 32(2), 192–198.

Tsing, A. L. 2015. *The Mushroom at the End of the World: On the Possibility of Life in Capitalist Ruins*. Princeton, NJ: Princeton University Press.

Valentine, J. 2004. "Sanctuary." In *Door in the Mountain: New and Collected Poems 1965–2003*. Middletown, CT: Wesleyan University Press.

Walcott, D. 1993. *Selected Poetry*. Vol. 15. Heinemann.

Webb, D. 2003. "On Friendship: Derrida, Foucault, and the Practice of Becoming," *Research in Phenomenology*, 33(1): 119–140.

Weeks, K. 2011. "Introduction." In *The Problem with Work: Feminism, Marxism, Anti-Work and Post-Work Imaginaries*, 1–36. Durham, NC: Duke University Press.

Williams, R. 1977. *Marxism and Literature*. Oxford, UK: Oxford Paperbacks.

Williams, R., and M. Orrom. 1954. *Preface to Film*. London: Film Drama.

Zigon, J. 2017. "A Politics of Worldbuilding—Cultural Anthropology." December 5. Retrieved from https://culanth.org/fieldsights/1249-a-politics-of-worldbuilding

Films

Khan, M., director, and H. Kalla, producer. 1988. *Dreams of Hind and Camelia*. Egypt: Egyptian Film Center.

Khan, M., director, and M. Zein, producer. 2005. *Downtown Girls*. Egypt: Oscar–El Nasr Films–El Masr.

Marker, C., director and producer. 1984. *2084*. West Germany: ISKRA

About the Author

Soha Mohsen is currently a first-year PhD candidate at the University of California, Davis. She earned the Andrew Mellon Huss-Lab post-MA fellowship in Fall 2019 and worked as adjunct faculty in the Department of Sociology, Egyptology, and Anthropology at the American University in Cairo in Spring 2019. This manuscript is based on her MA thesis in anthropology at the American University in Cairo.

CAIRO PAPERS IN SOCIAL SCIENCE

Volume Six

1   *The Political Economy of Revolutionary Iran*, Mihssen Kadhim
2   *Urban Research Strategies in Egypt*, Richard A. Lobban, ed.
3   *Non-alignment in a Changing World*, Mohammed el-Sayed Selim, ed.
4   *The Nationalization of Arabic and Islamic Education in Egypt: Dar al-Alum and al-Azhar*, Lois A. Aroian

Volume Seven

1   *Social Security and the Family in Egypt*, Helmi Tadros
2   *Basic Needs, Inflation and the Poor of Egypt*, Myrette el-Sokkary
3   *The Impact of Development Assistance on Egypt*, Earl L. Sullivan, ed.
4   *Irrigation and Society in Rural Egypt*, Sohair Mehanna, Richard Huntington, and Rachad Antonius

Volume Eight

1, 2   *Analytic Index of Survey Research in Egypt*, Madiha el-Safty, Monte Palmer, and Mark Kennedy

Volume Nine

1   *Philosophy, Ethics and Virtuous Rule*, Charles E. Butterworth
2   *The 'Jihad': An Islamic Alternative in Egypt*, Nemat Guenena
3   *The Institutionalization of Palestinian Identity in Egypt*, Maha A. Dajani
4   *Social Identity and Class in a Cairo Neighborhood*, Nadia A. Taher

Volume Ten

1   *Al-Sanhuri and Islamic Law*, Enid Hill
2   *Gone for Good*, Ralph Sell
3   *The Changing Image of Women in Rural Egypt*, Mona Abaza
4   *Informal Communities in Cairo: the Basis of a Typology*, Linda Oldham, Haguer el Hadidi, and Hussein Tamaa

Volume Eleven

1   *Participation and Community in Egyptian New Lands: The Case of South Tahrir*, Nicholas Hopkins et al.
2   *Palestinian Universities under Occupation*, Antony T. Sullivan
3   *Legislating Infitah: Investment, Foreign Trade and Currency Laws*, Khaled M. Fahmy
4   *Social History of an Agrarian Reform Community in Egypt*, Reem Saad

117

Volume Twelve

1 *Cairo's Leap Forward: People, Households, and Dwelling Space*, Fredric Shorter
2 *Women, Water, and Sanitation: Household Water Use in Two Egyptian Villages*, Samiha el-Katsha et al.
3 *Palestinian Labor in a Dependent Economy: Women Workers in the West Bank Clothing Industry*, Randa Siniora
4 *The Oil Question in Egyptian-Israeli Relations, 1967–1979: A Study in International Law and Resource Politics*, Karim Wissa

Volume Thirteen

1 *Squatter Markets in Cairo*, Helmi R. Tadros, Mohamed Feteeha, and Allen Hibbard
2 *The Sub-culture of Hashish Users in Egypt: A Descriptive Analytic Study*, Nashaat Hassan Hussein
3 *Social Background and Bureaucratic Behavior in Egypt*, Earl L. Sullivan, el Sayed Yassin, Ali Leila, and Monte Palmer
4 *Privatization: The Egyptian Debate*, Mostafa Kamel el-Sayyid

Volume Fourteen

1 *Perspectives on the Gulf Crisis*, Dan Tschirgi and Bassam Tibi
2 *Experience and Expression: Life among Bedouin Women in South Sinai*, Deborah Wickering
3 *Impact of Temporary International Migration on Rural Egypt*, Atef Hanna Nada
4 *Informal Sector in Egypt*, Nicholas S. Hopkins, ed.

Volume Fifteen

1 *Scenes of Schooling: Inside a Girls' School in Cairo*, Linda Herrera
2 *Urban Refugees: Ethiopians and Eritreans in Cairo*, Dereck Cooper
3 *Investors and Workers in the Western Desert of Egypt: An Exploratory Survey*, Naeim Sherbiny, Donald Cole, and Nadia Makary
4 *Environmental Challenges in Egypt and the World*, Nicholas S. Hopkins, ed.

Volume Sixteen

1 *The Socialist Labor Party: A Case Study of a Contemporary Egyptian Opposition Party*, Hanaa Fikry Singer
2 *The Empowerment of Women: Water and Sanitation Initiatives in Rural Egypt*, Samiha el Katsha and Susan Watts
3 *The Economics and Politics of Structural Adjustment in Egypt: Third Annual Symposium*

4   *Experiments in Community Development in a Zabbaleen Settlement*, Marie Assaad and Nadra Garas

Volume Seventeen
1   *Democratization in Rural Egypt: A Study of the Village Local Popular Council*, Hanan Hamdy Radwan
2   *Farmers and Merchants: Background for Structural Adjustment in Egypt*, Sohair Mehanna, Nicholas S. Hopkins, and Bahgat Abdelmaksoud
3   *Human Rights: Egypt and the Arab World, Fourth Annual Symposium*
4   *Environmental Threats in Egypt: Perceptions and Actions*, Salwa S. Gomaa, ed.

Volume Eighteen
1   *Social Policy in the Arab World*, Jacqueline Ismael and Tareq Y. Ismael
2   *Workers, Trade Union and the State in Egypt: 1984–1989*, Omar el-Shafie
3   *The Development of Social Science in Egypt: Economics, History and Sociology; Fifth Annual Symposium*
4   *Structural Adjustment, Stabilization Policies and the Poor in Egypt*, Karima Korayem

Volume Nineteen
1   *Nilopolitics: A Hydrological Regime, 1870–1990*, Mohamed Hatem el-Atawy
2   *Images of the Other: Europe and the Muslim World before 1700*, David R. Blanks et al.
3   *Grass Roots Participation in the Development of Egypt*, Saad Eddin Ibrahim et al.
4   *The Zabbalin Community of Muqattam*, Elena Volpi and Doaa Abdel Motaal

Volume Twenty
1   *Class, Family, and Power in an Egyptian Village*, Samer el-Karanshawy
2   *The Middle East and Development in a Changing World*, Donald Heisel, ed.
3   *Arab Regional Women's Studies Workshop*, Cynthia Nelson and Soraya Altorki, eds.
4   *"Just a Gaze": Female Clientele of Diet Clinics in Cairo: An Ethnomedical Study*, Iman Farid Bassyouny

Volume Twenty-one
1   *Turkish Foreign Policy during the Gulf War of 1990–1991*, Mostafa Aydin
2   *State and Industrial Capitalism in Egypt*, Samer Soliman
3   *Twenty Years of Development in Egypt (1977–1997): Part I*, Mark C. Kennedy
4   *Twenty Years of Development in Egypt (1977–1997): Part II*, Mark C. Kennedy

3 *Femininity and Dance in Egypt: Embodiment and Meaning in al-Raqs al-Baladi*, Noha Roushdy
4 *Negotiating Space: The Evolution of the Egyptian Street, 2000–2011*, Dimitris Soudias

Volume Thirty-three
1 *Masculinities in Egypt and the Arab World: Historical, Literary, and Social Science Perspectives*, Helen Rizzo, ed.
2 *Anthropology in Egypt 1900–1967: Culture, Function, and Reform*, Nicholas S. Hopkins
3 *The Church in the Square: Negotiations of Religion and Revolution at an Evangelical Church in Cairo*, Anna Jeannine Dowell
4 *The Political Economy of the New Egyptian Republic*, Nicholas S. Hopkins, ed.

Volume Thirty-four
1 *Egyptian Hip-Hop: Expressions from the Underground*, Ellen R. Weis
2 *Sports and Society in the Middle East*, Nicholas S. Hopkins and Sandrine Gamblin, eds.
3 *Organizing the Unorganized: Migrant Domestic Workers in Lebanon*, Farah Kobaissy
4 *The Food Question in the Middle East*, Malak S. Rouchdy and Iman A. Hamdy, eds.

Volume Thirty-five
1 *Oral History in Times of Change: Gender, Documentation, and the Making of Archives*, Hoda Elsadda and Hanan Sabea, eds.
2 *International Migration in the Euro-Mediterranean Region*, Ibrahim Awad, ed.
3 *Understanding the Public Sector in Egyptian Cinema: A State Venture*, Tamara C. Maatouk